Bergeners

TOMAS ESPEDAL

Bergeners

TRANSLATED BY JAMES ANDERSON

LONDON NEW YORK CALCUTTA

Seagull Books, 2017

© Gyldendal Norsk Forlag AS, 2013 (All rights reserved)

English translation © James Anderson, 2017

ISBN 978 0 8574 2 442 6

British Library Cataloguing-in-Publication Data

A catalogue record for this book is available from the British Library.

Typeset by Seagull Books, Calcutta, India

Printed and bound by Maple Press, York, Pennsylvania, USA

Just as the River Gaular sweeps past Sygna and narrows to a waist, suddenly cascading into a wide, powerful waterfall, so strong and foaming white that the river no longer resembles water but looks like a falling mountain, you can see Storehesten rising to a high, bluff summit, as if the peak is collapsing and reaching up at the same time, it's just an illusion; you see the mountain through shards of water splintering in the air. The boy stands on the slippery rocks just below the waterfall, its vapour sprinkling his face and hair, small droplets of moisture beading his jacket and trousers, and the water soaking him as he stands there in the sun. A pale rainbow above the falling water, above the waterfall that roars so loudly that he can hear no other voices above the voice of the water, it's calling to him. Now and then he sees a salmon launch itself in a high arc up the waterfall, inside the waterfall, as if the fish is searching for a place in the torrent which is still, a place where it can rest.

Where the fish can rest before it jumps further up the fall, until at last it leaps into the calm river water.

It seems impossible.

Roughly, the salmon is washed down by the weight of water, down to the bottom of the waterfall again, into the seething cauldron where the fish lies waiting. The boy watches the salmon make another attempt, a new jump into the wild water.

It seems impossible.

The boy begins to cry, tries to dry his tears with the arm of his jacket which is wet. Now he realizes that he's soaked, through his jacket and trousers, to his skin. He didn't mean to cry, he never cries, about anything, even about the worst things, never, but the mist from the waterfall trickles from his hair, down into his face and eyes.

New York City. The Standard Hotel. Room 1103. The loveliest room I'd ever seen. So transparent, so open, so white and severe. We stood in the doorway looking through glass across the bathroom and bedroom and lounge and through the windows to the city and the lights up high that were reflected back through the glass panes through the room to the doorway we stood in. The city was in the room. The room was in the city, like a transparent cube with glass walls. A hexagonal room with beds and pillows and duvets soft as wax. Light yellow curtains. A sofa bed upholstered in thick, grey woollen material. A brown leather chair. A large mirror. A plate-glass wall separating the bathroom with its shower and oval bathtub; egg white and with the rough texture of eggshell, so that everything in the room imitated nature, or was nature pressed together into a cube between other cubes in the city.

New York nature.

The streets criss-crossing beneath us. Fourteenth Street making a beeline for Union Square where there was a flower market. We filled the hotel room with flowers. They smelt sweet and heavy in the dark, and when we awoke in the morning, with the window open, we heard the buzzing of bees in the room.

New York night.

So light and mild. So sleepless and silent once the sounds had stretched out into the city and turned into a long, deep note of traffic and helicopters, sirens and hooters from ships on the Hudson River; we didn't hear them.

At night, when Janne was asleep, I would sit with my legs dangling out of the window of this tenth-floor hotel room and smoke. Sometimes, I'd suddenly be gripped by an irresistible impulse; I wanted to hurl myself out of the window. The thought was so overwhelming and powerful that I had to force myself to move away from the window, step by step towards the bed, lie down next to Janne and place her hand on my chest. Almost attaching myself to her. Spreading her hair across my face and entwining my legs in hers. Now I was secure. Now I was safe. I was firmly bound to her. I felt her calm breath, my pulse slowed, my heart beat normally; I could rest. But the following night it would happen again, I would sit alone at the window and be assailed by the thought that I'd never manage without her.

I didn't dare tell Janne about my fear of heights. How I'd inherited this fear from my mother, from the tenth floor in Skyttervei, how I'd regressed to my childhood elevation and my mother's fear of heights, how she dwelt within me with her phobias and anxiety, how I carried my mother about with me—I couldn't tell her that.

Janne wanted to go to the top of the Empire State Building. She wanted to go to the top of the Rockefeller Center. We went up in the lift, at terrific speed, while I fell down, I fell towards the floor of the lift. I clutched the Japanese woman standing next to me; she smelt of ginger and salt.

We took the lift to the seventeenth floor of the hotel to hear Edmund White giving a reading. He spoke of his lovers and read from his new book. The dust jacket had a photo of the author as a young man. He had dark, shoulder-length hair and a thick moustache, he was sporting a Whitmanesque hat. We were both disappointed at how heavy and old he was, at how fat and bloated he was, at how little he resembled his description of himself.

We met Frode and Gunnhild who were also at a literary festival in New York. Frode is a real cosmopolitan, he seems at home wherever he is. He knows how to sit and relax, and when to get up and leave. He knows how to talk, and how to keep quiet. Gunnhild has no sense of direction and never knows where she is. This is endearing, until you find yourself waiting for her, after she's wilfully and defiantly walked miles in the wrong direction.

As for me, I was wholly dependent on Janne. I didn't dare go anywhere without her, and when we were out and about in the city, I kept close to her, or I'd reach for her hand, although I noticed that she tried hard to conceal her hand, she'd put it in her jacket pocket, sometimes she'd hold it behind her back in an odd and affected manner.

I was frightened of being parted from her.

She found the right streets, buildings, she found the subway entrances and the trains we were to take, the stations we were to get off at, she found the places we were to see. She found the museums and bookshops, and when she wanted to pay the occasional visit to a clothes shop, or shoe shop, or department store, I'd stand at the entrance and wait for her.

I could stand waiting expectantly at the same spot for just as long as I needed to.

I shut my eyes, the sun shone, it fell on my face. I stood on the corner of Fifteenth Street and Sixth Avenue and waited for her for over an hour.

Then, she was back, emerging from the shop. Each time it was the same; I was filled with an immense and childlike joy, a scintillating happiness and profound gratitude—she was *my* girlfriend. And every time I saw her, after being parted from her, after waiting for her, I was on the brink tears but I managed hold them back, managed to hide it; she came out of the shop wearing a new white blouse, blue jeans and her tatty, old sandals.

We took the subway to Brooklyn and found The Unnameable, which one of Janne's friends had recommended to her. The bookshop wasn't large but it had the books we were looking for. Janne finally found *Nox* by Anne Carson. I found the Jennifer Moxley books I wanted. I stood in the recesses of the bookshop and stared at Janne. I could never look at her enough. I followed her with my eyes. Not letting her out of my sight. She tried to hide, disappeared behind a bookshelf. I followed her. It's lovely watching your girlfriend move among the bookshelves searching for the same books as you.

There's a bookshop near Union Square, The Strand, where we bought books by Peter Gizzi and Stacy Doris, Bill Luoma and Lee Ann Brown. My favourite poem, if it is a poem, is Bill Luoma's *My Trip to New York City*.

Fourteenth Street runs in a straight line from the Standard Hotel to Union Square. We walked it every day, up one side of the street, down the other, interrupted by regular halts at avenues: the traffic lights. Pedestrian crossings, a special rhythm of walking, move and stop, lights and cars. Janne wearing sunglasses, she said, There are so many beautiful people on the streets. She bent down and patted a dog on the head. The dog's ears were unnaturally short, and pointed, as if its ears had been cut or sharply chiselled; a hell hound. It launched itself at her face. The dog got tangled in her long hair, it snapped at her hair, tugged and tore at her long hair. Its owner yanked at its collar. What kind of dog is that, Janne shouted to the youth in baseball cap and trainers. He hauled the dog to him with all his strength: It's a pit bull, he said.

The following day, we'd seen the area around Ground Zero, there was a large gathering in Times Square. Flags were being waved and banners raised, there was singing and cheering, a great celebration: news had just come that Osama bin Laden had been shot at his home in Pakistan.

The breakfast room at the hotel was large and bright; an eternal summer garden of glass walls where the sunlight fell softly through light curtains, into the room with its white tablecloths. We ate scrambled eggs with toast and melted butter, drank coffee and orange juice. The counter had a flower arrangement on it, fresh, yellow daffodils. On the front page of the morning paper was a picture of Osama bin Laden. Written in bold, black type beneath the photo: May he rot in Hell.

That evening we finally managed to get into The Grill, the restaurant at the hotel, it was packed as usual but we got two places at the long counter in front of the grill itself; we sat with our backs to the guests in the restaurant and looked straight into the kitchen.

The heat from the grill was almost unbearable.

A fire of wood and charcoal glowed fiercely, a fire that flared up each time fat from the meat on the grill dripped into it. Seven men worked in the kitchen. They each had their allotted tasks and were overseen by the young chef who stood at the serving hatch and shouted. Three cods. Two bass. Two octos. One lamb. The young chef was awesome, shaven head, earrings, tattoos on his throat and down his arms. It looked as if he'd recently been in a fight, his left eye was bloodshot and there was a deep cut beneath the eye above the cheekbone. He sweated and shouted. He shouted most loudly and often at the apprentice at the big grill, the youth was being careless grilling his fish, the plump flesh was searing itself to the grill bars and he was trying to free it with a spatula. The chef hurried into the kitchen, stood next to the apprentice, thrust his hand into the flames of the grill and turned the pieces of fish by hand. He burnt himself but let his hand remain in the flames. It was a kind of exhibition, the chef could see that we were watching him. I felt a spontaneous fear each time I looked at the young chef, it was an instinct, an allure, but also pure dread, the sort I always feel when I'm attracted to something danger-ous. The chef put his hand in the fire. He was only a yard away from us, we who were drinking our wine, waiting for our food. He turned the pieces of fish with his hand, took his time over it, we could see that he was getting burnt, that his hand was red. We could smell his hand, how the smell of singed human flesh mingled with the smell of fish.

We'd ordered salmon. Grilled wild Norwegian salmon, it said on the menu. We were drinking a dry, white French wine. Janne was sweating. She took off her light jacket. The sweat ran down her face, gath-ered in a little hollow at the base of her neck, above her breasts.

It's funny to think that the fish we're going to eat swam about in a Norwegian fjord, I said, and maybe fought its way up a waterfall, before finally reaching the river where it was caught. And now it's ended up here, in a restaurant in New York, on our plates, I said.

Janne looked at me. Her eyes glistened in an odd way, as if she might be about to cry. But then she wiped her face with a napkin, drank some wine and straightened her back.

Tomas, she said. I don't know how to say this. I don't know if this is the right time to say it. I've waited and waited for the right opportunity, the right moment, but the right moment never seems to arrive, but as you said that about the salmon, I'll say this now: When we get home, we'll have to go our separate ways.

Jorge Luis Borges tells of a meeting with himself. The aged Borges is lying in a hotel room waiting for death. The younger one checks into the same hotel, only to discover that he's already registered—the same handwriting, the same name. He finds the old man in Room 19, just as he'd feared. The younger Borges fears this number, nineteen, he associates it with his past, and thus with death, which awaits him.

In my case, which isn't so alarming, or so literary, and perhaps more boring as a result, the number eleven is the one that constantly turns up, as if it's haunting me, and possibly signifies something, I don't know what. I was born in the eleventh month. I've written eleven books. Very often when I check in to a hotel I get a room with the number eleven in it: Room 211 recently in Tirana, Room 1103 before that in New York and, even more obviously, Room 11 here in Madrid. When I unlocked the door of this new room, a message already lay waiting on my bedside table. Written on a sheet of the hotel's notepaper. Hotel Embajada, Monday, 14 June, perhaps the message wasn't for me:

> We are invited to Kirsti tonight for dinner, at her house, please call me on 0034 622 783 734 for more details.
>
> Yours sincerely,
>
> Juan.

I knew nobody of that name. No Kirsti, either, it was odd that anyone even knew I was here, at this hotel, in Madrid. I had come to Madrid on impulse, to get away from the hubbub surrounding the publication of Knausgaard's books in Norway. He had mentioned my name in connection with an unpleasant episode in my flat, and my phone rang constantly, journalists from *Verdens Gang*, *Bergens Tidende*, *Dagbladet*, *Aftenposten*, Norwegian Broadcasting. I didn't know what to say to any of them, so I said I was on my travels. This was both true and untrue— I was hiding in Madrid.

I never phoned the number. I took off my clothes, opened the window and lay on the bed so that I could hear the street sounds right outside my window, I was on the ground floor. In the evening, I walked the streets at random, found a place to drink, lots of long mirrors in the narrow premises, like a corridor, with worn velvet sofas, small wooden tables, white-clad waiters, a largely male clientele, elderly men; I decided that this would be my regular haunt in Madrid.

I quickly got the feeling that I could disappear here in this corridor with all these old faces, these beautiful tables, these shiny-worn sofas, these walls of mirrors that reflected the backs and shoulders of the men who drank beer and smoked cigarettes. I could plainly see, in the mirror opposite my table, that I was in the process of becoming like the other men in the establishment, I was in the process of becoming everyone, in other words, I'd begun to resemble any man sitting at a table and eating alone, drinking alone, although I'm never alone when I get this feeling of solidarity, and of belonging: You find your place and disappear there, as quietly as you can.

'One morning when Gregor Samsa awoke from troubled dreams, he found that while in bed he had metamorphosed into a great, monstrous insect.'

A young man—he has lost or been robbed of his name—gets up early, it's Friday and the sun is shining, that's a good sign. He sleeps in the bedroom next to his mother's, it's not natural, he ought to find a flat of his own, a job, perhaps seek a lover or get himself some friends, but he doesn't want any of these things. He wants something different, he yearns for a greater transformation. He's always wanted a new face, another body and different clothes, anything other than the face and the life he's been forced to assume, and now at last he's mutating, it won't be long before he'll become someone else.

He'll get the body he desires, the arms he desires, he gets out of bed and drinks a glass of water, swallows the tablets. He needs a bigger and stronger body, a tougher body, the skin of his face is tightening now just the way he wanted and anticipated.

He's in the process of becoming himself.

It's a monstrous metamorphosis.

He's managed to create his own face, his own nose and mouth, his own expression. He has bleached his hair, expanded his body, he has made his own uniform.

He dresses himself, ordinary clothes, he doesn't want to attract attention, not yet, not too soon, later in the day he'll demonstrate who he's become. He folds his police uniform carefully into a bag. A gun, ammunition in a suitcase. Then, silently, he leaves the house.

It's clouded over, a heavy, grey layer has settled over the city which suddenly turns darker.

He gets into his vehicle, it's a van. A car bomb, he's made it himself. He's spent weeks at it, months, days and nights on a farm mixing chemicals. He's dried fertilizer, mixed and boiled diesel oil and crushed headache tablets. He's carried and pounded fertilizer. He's been poisoned by diesel fumes, despite his gas mask. He's had acid splashes and boils on his face and body; he's prayed to God that the great venture he's embarking on might succeed.

He's filled containers with the explosive. He's fitted the containers into the van, now he starts it up and drives, in towards the city centre. Many people already fill the streets, the shops, the offices, it's an ordinary Friday in July. Oppressively hot, overcast and sultry, soon it'll begin to rain.

He parks the van in the heart of the city, in the heart of all this normality, in the heart of all this everyday activity; then he leaves the van, he walks as normally as he can, as if he's just some ordinary guy in the city, but he's not.

At five minutes past five, the young man is on a ferry wearing a police uniform. One of the victims who survived the massacre on the island described him: a man in costume.

He stands on the ferry with a suitcase in one hand. The black costume with white high-visibility tape around the legs and arms is soaked with rain and sweat. He has made his costume and worked on it, and it arouses attention and suspicion as soon as he steps on to the island, perhaps he resembles one of those Hasmsunesque characters, so sensational and untimely in the place of their arrival; but it's no violin case the young man is carrying, in the suitcase is an automatic weapon and ammunition. He goes ashore. He brings no love with him, no mystery or unknown past, he arrives with pure present, with pure hate, he arrives on the island with a gun.

On the way up from the ferry dock to the main building on the island, he shoots the woman who comes to meet him.

He shoots the on-duty policeman as he emerges from the house.

He walks up to some high ground, a clearing in the forest, and shouts to the youngsters on the island to come to him. They move towards him from various directions and he begins to shoot. He shoots and shoots. He shoots and shoots and shoots. He goes round the island and shoots. He shoots and shoots and shoots and shoots. He re-loads and shoots. He searches and shoots. He shoots a fourteen-year-old. He shoots a sixteen-year-old. He shoots a seventeen-year-old girl. He shoots a nineteen-year-old boy. He shoots and kills sixty-nine teenagers on the island. The young man, who has lost or been robbed of his name, doesn't dare, or doesn't want to shoot himself. He wants to live. When the police finally get to the island and find him and shout to him, he is standing in the forest clearing with his hands above his head. He has just undergone a new and colossal change. He's become human. He behaves calmly and correctly. He is polite and cooperative; he's afraid of dying.

Thursday, 11 August: I wrote the short story 'A Man in Costume' almost in one go, over a couple of days. I hardly shut my eyes during those two days and nights, and in the short periods when I did sleep or doze, terrible nightmares came. It was as if I'd entered a zone of death, it wasn't good: it was a hellish zone. I battered and struggled and fought my way out of the zone, out of sleep. When I awoke, the remnants of the dream were in my bedroom: the insect with large wings thrashing about the room; I saw it large as life as I lay wide awake in bed.

Friday, 12 August: Today I find in the *Dictionnaire Infernal* that my insect is exactly like the illustration of Beelzebub. (The lord of the flies, or the lord of all that flies, or Satan himself.)

Sunday, 14 August: Something happened last night that's never happened before. I wrote till one-thirty in the morning, an entire short story, one of my best, I think, in one sitting. I must have fallen asleep around two at night and slept until two in afternoon today—twelve hours. It felt as if I'd been away for several months. A number of things were different in my bedroom; my bedside lamp wouldn't work, the bulb had burnt out. The bedroom door, which is always open, was shut or had blown to. The room smelt fusty, a faint scent of earth among the bed-clothes. I awoke and felt easier in my mind, and lighter, as if I'd lost or had something removed; it felt as if there was a vacuum in my breast, and it wasn't the least bit unpleasant.

The Love Disease   For Silje Aa. Fagerlund

An alcoholic's room.

Or a room for alcoholism.

It's a simple room. No furniture, only a bed and a writing table.

A lamp.

A balcony. View across a bay; it's a bay in Greece, on the mainland, in the south.

Between the balcony and the room there's an open veranda door, in the opening hangs a transparent piece of crocheted fabric, a white curtain with a light pattern of white leaves on a tree, I think it's a chestnut, it could be a beech.

Beneath the balcony stands a lemon tree.

The hum of the fan.

A warm wind that stirs the curtain, the white leaves of the chestnut billow in the wind.

It's both summer and winter in the room.

He can lie in bed all day and watch the white curtain that stirs in the wind.

It gives him a degree of comfort, a degree of peace to watch the white chestnut leaves that stir in the wind; it gives him a sensation of cold, of winter, of winter in the north. Outside it's summer, it's hot, it's bright August.

His hostess has placed an electric fan on the floor by the bed, it blows a cold, dry air which makes it possible to sleep at night, he sleeps during the day. Wakes and sleeps for short periods which coalesce into a long, unbroken half sleep or half wakefulness that lasts the whole day.

During the day he knows nothing but dreams.

During the day he knows only the lethargy the white, billowing curtain and the humming fan give him as a kind of comfort.

At night he's wakeful.

At night he knows only the loneliness that lies down beside him in the bed and keeps him awake.

At night he knows only this darkness that keeps him awake. He gets out of bed and sits on the balcony. He lights a cigarette. He drinks from the bottle under the chair. He looks over the roofs of the houses and the patios with garden flowers that glow faintly in the darkness, towards a stronger light in the harbour; an arc of light around the bay where cabin cruisers gleam reflecting street lamps and restaurants on the promenade. He's placed a small table on the balcony. Each night he sits in the dark and writes in a note-book. He can't see what he's writing. He scribbles down letters blindly, in the dark, the black letters vanish as soon as he writes them. He fills page after page, hour after hour, he writes to pass the time; he can neither see nor read what he writes.

The letters, the words, the sentences vanish as he writes them.

And he, the writer, vanishes too.

He's lived in the room at Nafplio for almost a month. He liked the room as soon as he saw it, as soon as his hostess opened the door and gestured towards the bed, the writing table and balcony—he'd found his room.

Every morning and evening, every day he does the same. In the morning, before sunrise, he takes the path over the hilltop to the beach on the other side of the mountain. He undresses and dives into the sea. Swims. Far out, so far that he begins to fear that he won't be able to swim back. He turns in the water, floats on his back and rests. Then he swims back, back towards the beach. He showers under ice-cold water. He rubs himself hard with a towel, gets dressed and takes the path through the pine trees, over the hill, to the village.

He has breakfast at Maria Helena's, it's just across the street from the guest house he's staying at.

Maria Helena is the most beautiful girl in the street, maybe in Nafplio, perhaps in the whole of Greece.

Everyone speaks her name, as often as they can.

Maria Helena!

Maria Helena!

Maria Helena, he says, I could do with a cup of coffee and a slice of bread and butter.

The paper boy, the postman, the schoolchildren, a woman dressed in black, a youth on a moped, they all go past and call out her name.

Maria Helena could be seventeen or eighteen, she's far too young to chase after her name like that.

She waits in her parents' cafe, runs and walks and almost skips between the tables. That morning, the first time she spoke to him—she'd asked him something, out of curiosity, naturally, but her question contained something more, an interest or attentiveness—he went to the barber's and got his hair cut. He shaved off his beard. He went to a clothes shop and bought a new white shirt, a pair of trousers and new sandals.

He's occupied his usual place at the table in the opening between outside and in; from where he's sitting he can see the family working in the cafe, the mother behind the counter, the father in the kitchen and Maria Helena darting between the tables, between the cars; there's a narrow, cobbled one-way street running past and partly through the cafe, as if the street is part of the family; people slam on their brakes, shout out of their car windows, ordering bread and coffee, buying and discussing, kissing and sending greetings, before driving on, walking on, a constant flow of passers-by. After he's eaten his bread, Maria Helena arrives with little cakes he hasn't ordered.

Try the one with almonds . . . the chocolate-chip one is nice . . . this one's lemon . . . and my father's baked this one with butter only . . .

He eats the cakes, dunks them in his coffee. When the plate is empty, Maria Helena asks him which cake he liked best, she always does this, every morning, even though his answer is always the same. The cake your father baked with butter only, that's the best, he says. Tomorrow you'll taste one that's even better, she says, it's something she says every morning.

After breakfast, he crosses the street and goes up to his room and gets into bed.

He succumbs to the weariness that's become such a big part of him; it grows and becomes weightier, that's how it feels, him getting thinner and smaller, the weariness getting heavier and larger, soon it'll fill him completely.

Weariness, lethargy, warmth.

For a little while he thinks about Maria Helena, he reads a book, drinks from the many bottles he's stashed in his room: wine, whisky, ouzo, gin and vodka, it doesn't matter what he drinks. He sinks into the apathy which imparts a kind of well-being, a pleasure, almost; he feels sorry for himself, he cries, he lights a cigarette. He carries on long conversations with a shadow. He rises from his bed, walks about the room. He forces the shadow down into a chair. I understand you, he says. You did the only thing that was right, it was necessary, he says to the shadow. He gets down on his knees, crawls around the floor. For a long time, he lies motionless on the hard floor, his head out of the veranda door. The sky is deep blue, a flock of doves flies in an arc over the balcony. He likes lying like this, as if he were dead, on his back, arms splayed out, legs at an unnatural angle on the carpet. When his body aches sufficiently, he gets back into bed. During the day he knows only this weariness that lies over him in his bed like a heavy animal or a great bird, it sits on his chest when he sleeps and when he wakes.

In the evenings, he eats at a restaurant, always the same restaurant. It stands, almost hidden, in the corner of the large, open square which forms the centre of Nafplio. It is a quiet square, surrounded by Venetian houses. You hardly hear the voices from the restaurants, the footsteps of the passers-by. He sits outside, beneath an awning in the twilight and watches the couples crossing the square, the way they embrace, kiss, fumble with one another's fingers. He usually has fish, with a bottle of white wine, smokes, orders ouzo and water, one glass after another. On some evenings, there's a small gypsy orchestra which plays to the restaurant's clientele: three men in black hats and dark shirts, worn, flared trousers, jewellery and earrings; he admires the gypsies for their coarseness and strength, the way they care so little about their teeth falling out, a missing finger, all the things they lose without worrying about it, seemingly, the way their bodies decay and fill out, yes, the way age ravages them without robbing them of their audacity and vital spark—they play and sing with gusto. One evening he sees Maria Helena passing by with some other girls. She spies him sitting hidden in the far corner of the restaurant and secretly turns to him and sends him a glance that troubles him. She gives him a long, provocative stare, then she turns sharply away, and her movement stays with him, it makes him uneasy, it gives him pain. She says something to her friends, they remain close to his table for a while, speaking softly and laughing, it's obvious they're talking about him. Then they move on, across the square, noisy and brutal; he sees how she's about to disappear among the houses, follows her back with his eyes, her back and hair and the long legs that walk, he almost calls after her, he almost stands up and calls, but instead he crumples into his chair and mumbles to himself. Now he can't have his breakfasts with Maria Helena any more. It was his only joy in Nafplio, what got him out of bed in the mornings. The next day he packs his few belongings in his rucksack, walks through the morning-still town and takes a seat in the bus station's waiting room, to take a bus onwards, southwards.

De Profundis   For Monica Aasprong

My last love affair: cigarettes.

Smoking and writing, it's the same action, but in opposite directions and with opposite effects and using opposite hands.

To smoke. To write in the air.

The cigarette's black characters.

To love someone who's gone, that's what writing is.

To write is love unto death.

In the deepest blackest sorrow in black

sorrow black the deepest black

sorrow black and deep

the deep blackest sorrow

deep black

deep

so deep so black so deepblack

so blackdeep so black is sorrow

like being imprisoned in light.

Did darkness become light?

No, darkness didn't become light

not light not brighter not brighter light

not light not brighter not light or brighter

light

it turned black

the darkness turned black

nothing is blacker than deep sorrow

nothing darker than the blackest sorrow.

In the deepest black sorrow

I was imprisoned in light

so bright that I was close to disappearing

a disappearance almost

directly into the light

which vanished.

Pinturas Negras   **For Josefine Klougart**

In June 2010, I went to Madrid. I got a room at the
Hotel Embajada, number eleven, on the ground floor.
A book fair was being held in Madrid; I was to give
a reading, one of three Norwegian writers, but I
hadn't been told who the other two were. On the

first morning, when I went down to the breakfast room, Dag Solstad was seated at one of the tables. I didn't know him but felt almost obliged to sit at the same table, anything else would have seemed unnatural. There were lots of things I wanted to ask him about but I didn't dare. He sat there, formidable, in a chalk-white suit and white shirt unbuttoned down his chest. His white, curly hair fell wild and unkempt into his pale face. He was completely white and the sun shone in through the window of the breakfast room. It was like sharing a table with a ghost, or an author from some bygone age, one of the classic authors, one of the dead authors, and I didn't know what to say to this character who was so timeless and grotesque. For some reason, I let it be known that I was reading Thomas Mann's diaries in German. Yes, Thomas Mann wrote his diary every evening before he went to bed, said Dag Solstad. Every evening without fail that diary had to be written, every evening, every single evening before he went to bed. Why didn't he just go to bed, roared Dag Solstad suddenly.

The white suit and the white hair shone in the dark; he crossed the traffic-filled streets of Madrid without glancing left or right. He launched himself into the traffic, walked straight across as if the street belonged to him and his freedom or fearlessness; I couldn't understand what drove him to cross the road in that lethal manner. I grasped his elbow and tried to steer him across Calle de Alcalá: Don't you feel frightened at all? I asked. I used to keep goal for Sandefjord FC, and a keeper can't be frightened, he said. I wasn't a good goalkeeper. Albert Camus was a better keeper than me, but I'm a better writer than him, Dag Solstad said.

I informed Dag Solstad that I wanted to see Goya's 'Pinturas negras'—Black Paintings—in the Prado Museum. Well, if you want to view Goya's Black Paintings in the Prado, you've got to walk straight through the first rooms without turning your head. You mustn't stop or look at a single painting. Just go through as fast as you can with blinkers on, all the way to the innermost room of the museum. That's where Goya's Black Paintings are on display. After you've seen them, you must leave the museum immediately, in just the same manner as you came in, Dag Solstad said.

A few days later, I did precisely as Dag Solstad had directed. I walked quickly past the first rooms in the Prado Museum without turning my head. I didn't stop or look at a single painting. Not a glance at Velázquez's paintings which I'd wanted to see for a long time, not so much as a peek at *Las Meninas* which would probably have been my favourite painting and which I passed at high speed with my hands cupped like blinkers to the sides of my face. I walked as quickly as I could to the innermost room of the museum. Here were the Black Paintings by Goya. I've never seen anything like them. The first thing I felt was that I wanted to quit the room immediately, that I was looking at something I shouldn't be seeing and that maybe wasn't even meant to be seen: Goya had painted the pictures on the walls of his cellar in the house he'd bought outside Madrid, the House of the Deaf, La Quinta del Sordo. And what did the paintings portray—was it dreams, nightmares, visions of something evil, of something black that was looming, or already there, I didn't want to know, didn't want to see what I was seeing and I walked restlessly between the pictures, those black pictures, until I managed to tear myself away and get out of the exhibition room, comparatively unharmed, I hoped. But that night, I underwent a terrible change. I struggled and resisted the whole night; I clasped my hands, whispered and prayed, shouted and wept, and when the light of morning finally arrived and I managed to get out to the bathroom to look at myself in the mirror, it was a shock to find I looked just as I had done before, it was impossible to tell that I wasn't myself any longer.

The Diaries   **For Rita Labrosse**

Why don't I just go to bed.

The part of Madrid I've ended up in, close to Plaza de Colón, is hideous and grey: traffic-laden streets and avenues squeezed between greyish-black facades and dirty windows with no view of sea or river, no trees, no park, nothing natural, only city that reflects city in a thin layer of exhaust fumes and street dust.

I like it here.

Sitting on a street corner, watching, smoking and watching, watching and drinking wine, sitting the whole day and watching the throng of people that streams past, a fast-flowing and calming river of humanity; you feel the pleasant sensation of drowning, of being carried by the current towards still waters.

It's not hard to disappear in a city.

In the evenings I'm back at my regular haunt: Santa Barbara. I need her. I don't know whose patron saint she is, but it must be the lonely and the drinkers who pray to her. What do we pray for? More wine. More cigarettes. Something to eat. That's all. Someone to talk to, someone to love? No, right now I'm better off on my own with the cigarettes and wine.

External ugliness is outweighed by the beauty within; red plush sofas, wooden tables, glasses and bottles, mirrors, women, cigarette smoke, waiters in white, male waiters. In Madrid I want to disappear indoors.

Am I wanted? Inside the bar, it's almost completely dark.

Finn Bjørn Tønder rings me from Bergenes Tidende. He's read Karl Ove's fifth volume and refers to me several times as a torpedo. He's a crime journalist. Hasn't got the vocabulary. And works in the cultural section of the paper.

People phone from *Bergensavisen*, *Bergenes Tidende*, *Dagbladet*, *Aftenposten*, *Verdens Gang* and Norwegian Broadcasting. Linn Rottem calls from the House of Literature in Oslo and asks if I'll come and give a reading from my diaries. Well, it's a good literary idea. I reply that I don't keep a diary.

It's not necessary to commit a crime to become a criminal.

To be confined in a city, imprisoned, captive, in a large prison to be sure, but a city is only as big as the restraint that envelops you.

You see lots of beautiful women here, but also beautiful men. Eat tarta de Santiago and drink coffee in my hotel room.

Black coffee, like an injection of amphetamines, of caffeine, of nicotine, of heroin, my love.

Sit at the little writing table that I've pushed over to the window; the window opens like a door, you open the door and look out over a large, open square. There are benches in the square and trees, al fresco dining beneath red canopies, you hear voices and watch people come and go, crossing the square, alone or in pairs, in groups, a group of friends and girlfriends, families, once an entire class of schoolchildren in uniform, white shirts and black trousers, white blouses and black skirts, and the small, black heads bent to one another and making a shrill, bright sound that filled the square, until the teacher blew a whistle and there was silence. Then you could hear the wind again, the wind in the tree-tops, you could hear the birds and the cars in the distance and the subdued voices of the people dining outside which now and then were cut off by a passing beggar: he took his stand by the outermost table and, in a cracked, weepy voice, sang out his story.

He sang, and the voices in the restaurant were stilled, the eating ceased, everything was halted and darkened by this song, the entire square was affected by the song as if caught up in an accident. The beggar sang and the light left the square. It went dark. The square was in darkness, maybe it was a cloud blocking out the sun, maybe it was a flock of crows, every evening several hundred crows flew in a great mass across the square, perhaps it was just imagination, but the singer sang, and for several minutes the square was bereft of light.

A young couple, yawning simultaneously as they walk past.

The sudden, violent rain shower beating against the lamp posts, and the light globes giving off a shining, white steam.

Eat roast chestnuts and drink a bottle of Rioja. Make notes and write: The man in the window.

New title: The man who loved everything.

The chestnut, once the shell has been crushed and the nut exposed, is shaped like a heart. A heart covered in feathers, that's what the flesh of the chestnut looks like.

When all the chestnuts have been opened, the shells lie strewn over the thick wax paper and look like a plucked bird.

The Spanish police: tall, black boots, loose trousers, stiff, blue shirts, black belts, with those leather holsters containing on the left a rubber truncheon, a revolver on the right of the belt, black gloves (to avoid leaving fingerprints? to stop tainted blood getting on the hands?); they're well dressed and brutal, these young boys in uniform.

The beggar drinks openly from a bottle of spirits in a corner of the square, he stands under a tree. Then, unsteadily, he crosses towards the outermost table of the restaurant terrace, he pulls himself up, lifts his head, puts one hand to his breast and sings out his song, his story.

In the background, far away, it seems, we hear disturbing noises, faint, but then growing in volume, slowly, like a storm, a thunderstorm bearing down on the square; wind or rain, or is it the sound of drums? Drums being beaten, feet pounding? The diners become uneasy, the policemen tense, their voices raised, suddenly one of them hurls himself at the beggar, hits him in the face, knocks him to the ground and rolls him over so that he's face down on the ground. His arms are pinioned behind his back, the handcuffs are put on and he's dragged by the legs across the square, hauled up and pushed into the back of a police van.

We hear the rumpus approaching, voices shouting, the thud of drums, the throwing of stones, glass smashing. And suddenly we see the crowd marching behind red flags and white banners. A large, lengthy demonstration, thousands of open mouths and angry eyes, as if an entire population is on the move with demands for change and revolution.

It came to me, perhaps it was in a dream, the night after I'd seen Goya's Black Paintings, that they contained the answer to a riddle, if you read them right. But could hundred-and-ninety-year-old paintings reveal something about what happened eight months ago? The first painting, if you imagine yourself descending the steps to a cellar, Goya's cellar, and glancing to the left, the way you start reading a page from the left, the first sentence, or first painting you saw, would be a picture of a dog. This dog has been construed as a self-portrait of Goya. The dog appears to be falling into an abyss, its eyes tell you that it's racked by despair, by a sorrow, these must be the saddest eyes in the history of art. Directly opposite this picture, on the right, and thus the last picture in the room—I don't want to mention the pictures in-between just yet, let's call them a vision, Goya's black nightmare—is the portrait of a woman. It's generally accepted that this is a portrait of the woman with whom Goya had a relationship in the final years of his life: Leocadia Zorrilla. In the painting, she's young and pretty, dressed in black and with a black veil over her face. Is she in mourning because the painter, Goya, is dead? She isn't sad, it looks as if she may be in a reverie, may be bored, preoccupied, well, what is she thinking about? She stares blankly towards the sick dog. The dog that's falling, it will die, and she will live on.

I met Maud Kennedy at Cafe Opera in Bergen. I was standing in the bar with Preben Jordal, something I did often, at one time, I liked listening to him running down Norwegian writers and Norwegian literature. He'd stolen my girlfriend and had just trashed my best friend's new anthology in *Klassekampen*, but I liked Preben, the way I often like harsh and imma-ture men. D'you remember, not so very long ago, how we used to lap up and lionize Thomas Bernhard, and now we don't even bother picking up one of his books, or reading a sentence Thomas Bernhard wrote? Preben said to me in the bar of the Cafe Opera. While we were talking, while Preben was talking and rubbishing Thomas Bernhard—whom we'd both thoroughly enjoyed and who we now couldn't stomach any more, perhaps because he was so easy to imitate, perhaps because he had such a

strong and deleterious influence on a number of
Norwegian authors, and because he wrote what
Peter Handke called impoverished prose—while
Preben was going on about all this, a girl with long
plaits and a red leather jacket approached us in the
bar. She positioned herself between us, between
Preben and me, and he left, out of politeness or
pique, and took the stairs to the first floor. I stood
alone with the stranger, it was impossible to tell how
old she was, she was made up like a young girl and
had done her long hair in two plaits. This was a
lonely and dark period of my life, and I began to
think of a short story by Alberto Moravia about the
devil: he could assume any guise, any character, and
he could turn into precisely the character his victim
most craved, in my case, a woman. She was wearing
a red leather jacket and in her hand was a red leather
bag. She showed me the contents of her bag. She
was wearing bright, red lipstick, red bootees, she'd
dressed up as a prostitute. When the lights were
flicked off and on and time was called at Cafe Opera,
she asked me if I'd go back to her studio with her.
She was a painter, she said. She had drink and music
at her studio, she said, and I went with her.

Maud and I turned out of C. Sundtsgate towards
Tollboden where the whores stood waiting for cus-
tom. Nigerian girls, dark, scared, contorted faces
with large white eyes, terrified or empty, without

light, just these white eyeballs in the shadowy faces hidden beneath shawls and caps; they resembled the women in the painting by Goya, the one called *The Great Billy-Goat*, one of the Black Paintings in which the women sit huddled in a group before the great, black creature that is a man in animal costume and a goat-mask, a human animal; here he had come and stood in front of the prostitutes who smoked and listened to what he wanted to do with them, we could view the scene from the window of Maud's studio. Maud took her clothes off. She pulled on a pair of paint-flecked white overalls. She was no longer a prostitute, she was an artist. I was to see her change character several times; she could be a business-woman, mother, daughter, victim, lover, seducer, whatever suited the moment best, now she was a painter.

The next day I regretted it more than I'd ever regret-ted anything, but the next time we met, I went with her again.

I quickly became dependent on her. And as I began to display emotions, the first evening I said I needed her, that I wanted to see her again, she took pains to let me know how many men she'd dated, and how many men she continued to date, she reeled off a whole list of names, names of men I knew, a priest, a musician, a writer, a painter, and a lot of names I didn't know, it was a long list of names, and now I was one of the names.

She enjoyed seeing me enraged, jealous, despairing.

She enjoyed seeing me weak, it did her good, it made her strong.

I made up my mind not to meet Maud again. Then my phone began to ring at night, and one night when I answered it, I heard her voice in a contorted howl of wind and music and breaking glass, as if she were ringing from hell or a cellar where her voice reverberated from the walls before it disappeared and died out as a man's voice began to yell and weep into the phone.

The same thing the following night. The distorted voice from hell that snivelled and cried on the phone. Where was he calling from?

I dreamt and had nightmares. Then the phone rang. A drunken man's voice, though clearer now; he said his name was Frode Olson and that he was Maud's boyfriend and that he knew what I was doing to his girlfriend and how I did it to his girlfriend, he shouted it down the phone. Curses and swearing and sexual parts in a roaring tirade of English and Norwegian and an incomprehensible language that turned into snuffling and weeping and sometimes howls.

A wounded animal. A wild and wounded animal, a dog, a hound from hell.

I dreamt about this dog, had nightmares about the dog, I had to kill this dog.

I said this down the phone, at night, if you howl any more, I'll kill you.

Then it went quiet. For a long time things went quiet.

I met Maud again at Cafe Opera; I got hold of her and asked her who was phoning me at night. She looked at the floor, said she was sorry and said that Frode got off on stimulants, that he could be danger-ous, that he'd beaten her up, that he'd been found guilty of assaulting her, that he'd never been her boyfriend, that he terrorized those she'd been with. But why do you tell him who you've been with, and why give him our phone numbers? I knew she was doing it to destroy him. He forces me to, she said.

I'd seen them once, Frode and Maud, walking hand in hand through the city, it was quite a sight: he, tall with high-heeled cowboy boots, distressed jeans, a black leather jacket with no shirt underneath, sunglasses, long, thin hair plastered down and back with oil, he exactly resembled who he wanted to resemble, Nicolas Cage as Sailor in the film *Wild at Heart*, presumably they'd watched the film together, and Maud was something of a Lula in red leather jacket and black Levis, sunglasses, a ponytail, in their own way they made a fine couple, they were wild at heart, and they looked it as they walked like Lula and Sailor through the streets of Bergen.

Frode was a painter, many people considered him among the best of his generation, perhaps he was the one who painted most forcefully: large expressive pictures about violence and assault, often featuring grotesque male figures dressed in uniforms and soldiers' helmets, they fought and made war and fucked in a never-ending battle where expletives were yelled in capital letters sprayed on to the paintings like graffiti. Frode was beginning to break through as an artist, but while he was working frenetically on these big murals he was getting high on alcohol and pills and on Maud who had relationships with other men. She seemed, systematically, to screw men who were known or important in the city, and then she told Frode who phoned and terrorized them at night; it was his war, his fight. It was also his love, his sexuality, his high, he fought and painted; he was the man in the uniform and the soldier's helmet who howled and screamed, he screamed in his paintings, he screamed down the phone.

Frode wanted to be an artist, he was an artist, he wanted to be a real artist; he wanted to suffer, he wanted to fight, he wanted to feel pain, he wanted to get high, he wanted to live hard, he wanted to break barriers and be uncompromising, he was a romantic. Frode wanted to be a great and famous painter, and to get there he needed Maud.

Frode forces me to tell him who I've been with, Maud said to me at Cafe Opera. Did I feel sorry for her, had I become fond of her, did I need her? I put my arm round Maud. Pulled her towards me. Can we go home to yours? she asked.

I was standing at the bar with Herman and Karl Ove. Maud and I signalled that we wanted to be off and Herman and Karl Ove made it obvious that they wanted to come too, it wasn't unusual for them to come back to my place and continue the party. We walked together through the city; had Maud already been flirting with Herman and Karl Ove, it wasn't impossible, and I thought about it as we left Cafe Opera. But Maud is mine, I thought as we walked, crossing Torgallmenningen and the Fish Market and along Bryggen towards my flat in Dreggen. We took the lift up, it was as if we took the lift down, down to the basement, down to the depths, down into the darkness. We took the lift up and went into my flat. I don't recall what we talked about. We sat in my flat and gloom settled upon us. I got out all I had in the way of drink and cigarettes, we had music on loud, and it wasn't long before Maud was sitting next to Karl Ove on the sofa. It wasn't long before they both got up and went out of the living room, I was sure they were off to her place, Maud had gone off with Karl Ove. Herman said that Maud had been flirting with him and I confided to Herman that I had a relationship with Maud. Then we're a couple of idiots, no three, four idiots, we're all idiots, Herman said to me. It had begun to get light. Herman wanted to go home, I accompanied him to the door. Safe journey, Herman, I said, we're all idiots, I laughed, but there was nothing to laugh about, when I opened my bedroom door to get undressed and go to bed, Maud was lying there weeping with her clothes all ripped around her.

I lent Maud a shirt and some underwear. I made breakfast. Maud couldn't, wouldn't explain what had happened. She phoned a girlfriend who collected her in a taxi. That was the last time I saw Maud. But only a few days later, during the night, the phone rang. It was Frode. Your mate, the author, he shouted, raped my girlfriend in your flat. Frode, Maud isn't your girlfriend, I said. And it wasn't rape, otherwise the rest of us would have heard it, we would have heard Maud scream, and we heard nothing, Frode. If you want to talk to me, you come up here, during the day, sober, you know where I live. He said nothing more, but didn't hang up, I heard that terrible hellish humming, a heavy, dark background music and sudden roars, howls and sounds of glass breaking, furniture and objects being dragged across the floor, thumps and bangs, it occurred to me that perhaps he was painting, that this was the way he worked in his studio, high, with his mobile in one hand and a paint brush in the other.

Next day Karl Ove phoned. There's a bloke phoning me, us, at night, I don't know who he is but he's ranting on about me having raped his girlfriend. He rings non-stop during the day and several times each night on the landline, my marriage is on the rocks, Karl Ove said. I'll deal with him, I replied. I'll see him and get him to stop phoning. I called Maud, several times, but she didn't answer.

That night Frode rang. I waited until he was finished with his accusations and threats, roaring and cursing, shrieking and shouting, until he was expectant and silent, then I said clearly and calmly, Listen carefully, Frode. I know where you're ringing from. If you phone me or Karl Ove once more, I'll come straight over to your studio and smash your mobile phone and then I'll break both your arms and give you the pasting you deserve.

Then things calmed down again, at last things were quiet. I heard nothing from Maud, nothing from Frode, or from Karl Ove. And in this silence I descended into a circle of hell full of feelings of guilt and angst; I couldn't sleep in my own bed, moved into the living room, lay on the sofa in there night after night with dark visions that kept me awake. And when I did finally sleep, in brief snatches, I dreamt of humanoid creatures that flew and floated around in a semi-darkness struggling and fighting, raping and consuming one another. And in the midst of the dream, always, the fear of not waking up: Now you're dying, you're already dead. And here in death it's not the end, here in death life is a battle in which we bite into faces and arms, eat our way down to intestines and kidneys, hearts and lungs, consume and are consumed, ceaselessly, without end.

I was waiting for a calamity. It arrived in the spring. Frode died. He was found on the floor of his studio. I got the message via a withheld number on my mobile phone. I learnt that Maud had moved to Gothenburg. I knew that Karl Ove lived there already. In May, the fifth volume in his novel series came out, and in it he spoke of the rape accusations and what, according to him, had taken place in my flat. I was forced to go away, and bought a plane ticket to Madrid. Here I saw the Black Paintings by Goya. The night after I'd seen the pictures, it came to me, as if in a dream, that the paintings held the answer to Frode's death.

Maud was Frode's Leocadia Zorrilla.

The dog—that's me.

Rome Days   **For Matilda Roos**

The pigeons grey lighter grey and greyer grey and darker grey and some almost white. But the loveliest pigeons are grey.

Like silver   gleaming silver.
Grey-grey and glossy. Gradations of grey which are lighter and darker rings around the body that are silver and waves in feathers and wings. There's nothing more beautiful than pigeons.   When they fly.
The pigeons open their wings and launch themselves from cobbles fold their feet under their stomachs and fly   small claps
in the city   between the house walls
above the river above the rise high above the trees and streets and people   which is you

Grey tears spill greyly over the soft eye's edge the eye's arc of stone is sprinkled with water that falls on water in the eyeball.   Rome's fountains.

Weeping's eye.

Grey trees at crack of dawn.   Rome's stone pines.

Grey trees in a thin row of shadows. Misty, distant figures that will not vanish.

High stretching swaying sylphlike trunks with heavy
crowns of needles   pricking
sprouting so maliciously   so high
that the birds fly   beneath

Between the stone pines   the city
Rome   sheltered
by the trees.   Roma
the city with that remarkable name   Amor.

In the evening, at sunset, friends gather under the trees on the Aventine Hill. People talk in hushed tones, as if they're indoors. The sun goes down. The sun sets fire to the roofs of the houses and the cupolas and trees that surround the city. People put their arms round each other. And darkness falls. When you stand on a hill above the city under the trees in the evening, you can sense the deep fear that one day the darkness will be total.

From the window of the room at Hotel S. Anselmo, on the second floor, you can see right into a lime tree. It's as if you're sitting behind the curtain to expose the tree's secret. One of its branches grows towards the window and scratches the pane when the wind blows. If the window was kept open, the branch would grow into the hotel room. The lime-tree branch would spread inside the room, its leaves would unfurl, it would turn to winter, spring, and there, hidden behind the curtain, you imagine how the tree and the seasons would take over the empty room.

Just where the Tiber twists and surges under the oldest bridge, the moving water meets an opposing current, and it's no longer possible to tell which way the river's flowing. On a shelf of rock beneath the bridge is a damaged tree, thin, new branches reach out from the rotten trunk.

Night-time trees along the river. Dark, deep grey with black leaves the trees stand black and wakeful.

You never dream about trees.

Albergo del Sole   Campo de' Fiori

Change hotels. Move out of the S. Anselmo on the
Aventine Hill to the Albergo del Sole at Campo de'
Fiori. Get a dingy little room with a view of a back-
yard. Like living in a cramped, black box. Hot without light. A well-deserved room. As if the receptionist
is a stern and smartly dressed Dante: I'm banished
to the darkness with the lovers.

A square, black room that sinks or is hauled down
into the depths, the way the ancient lift in the hotel
often ends up in the basement.

A sleepless night among shadows.

How do you ascend from here, get out of here?

Clasp my hands, pray for light, but it gets darker. No,
it can't get any darker, it's gone completely black.
What should you do when it's completely black?
Turn on the bedside lamp and the artificial light is
choked as if hasn't got enough oxygen. As if the
darkness is oozing out of my pores and choking all
the light and air in the room.

The black room. The darkness comes from within.

The internal darkness is darker than the external darkness, the external darkness blends with the internal.

Don't let go here, don't hold tight, sink deeper into the darkness, into the night.

Is this the last night? Some night must be the last, is this the one, this night, now? Now tonight, is this the end? Here in the darkness, in the black box sunk in the depths, deep in the night, is it the end? Is the end now? Is the end here? Here in the room, here in the dark, here in the night, now? Now and here, here in the room, the last night?

No.

No.   No.

Knee-bend.   Kneel.

Knees.   Down.

Yes   and   yes   and   yes   and   woe   and   woe
and   woe   and   yes   and   yes   and   yes.

Change hotel rooms   Am given

a large, bright double with a view of the flower market   Campo de' Fiori. Chrysanthemums.
Gladioli. Roses. Tulips. Lilies. Sunflowers and honey-
suckle.   It smells like
spring and autumn   In the room.

At last I've got the light I need
To go to sleep.   The scent
of flowers   the sound of voices   and footsteps
from the flower market   in the room
in my dream   Apollo and Daphne
one loves and the other won't be loved.

Daphne runs and Apollo runs after her. They run. We
run. You run and I run after you. Apollo runs after
Daphne. They run through the forest, along the river,
we run through the city, I run after you. Almost grab
your hair, that long hair which you lose. You run
without hair and increase speed, how fast you run,
don't you know who I am? I'm Apollo, I'm running
after you. You're running so fast, I increase speed.
Almost grab your arm, your hand which you lose.
You're running and weeping. I run, we run through
the city, out of the city, over the bridge, over the river,
I can hear your breathing becoming laboured, it will
run out, you'll lose your breath. You lose your hair,
lose your arm. You're breathing so heavily, so deeply,
you're nothing but breath. Soon now your breath
will cease. Daphne. Daphne. If you stop now, I'll hug
you like a tree.

Rome days   white. Grey
Hot   bright   blue.
Thick blue curtains a blue   sunlight
Numbing askew in blue   in the room.

At last I've got the light I need
To be able to write   Read
Emily Dickinson   at night
the shiny white poems that light up   in the darkness
on the third floor balcony with its view over the deserted
flower market   the silent streets   and the sky
above a darkened sleeping Rome.   In some places
it's better to sleep during the day   be awake
at night.   Sometimes
it's better to write without light in the dark when
the black characters vanish as you write them. Like
writing in water. The way the words float off on the
white in the blackness; you can't read what you've
just written. Daphne. Janne. I dream of a transformation.   It's not hard to love trees a
tree nor flowers a flower nor rivers a river or stone
stones and water that falls runs shines in the streets
in the cities the city and the people here the faces
there.

                              It's not hard
to love women a woman nor a man old or young the
clothes he wears with such difficulty such ease. A
child a dog the dogs the gardens the balconies the
houses. It's not hard

to love a home   What's difficult
my love   is loving you.

The pigeons grey lighter grey and greyer grey and
darker grey and some nearly white. And there, so
alarming and suddenly flying out of a hole in the
church wall, a white pigeon,
completely   white.

Light conditions

Ah, the colour blue. Isn't it pretty, isn't it deep, isn't
it oppressive, how light it is.

It seems so weightless, the blue colour, when you see
it above the house where you live.

At night. During the day. In the evening. In the morning in the sunlight, in the dark, something burning
blue.

Dark blue, light blue.

We can't say that blue is now blue. We can't say that
love is now dead. I can't say that I'm alive.

I'm alive. In something blue. So blue that it's nearly dark. So blue that it's nearly dead.

Ah, blue. What happens to the colours when they go out?

Isn't it wonderful how blue the sea is. At night it's black.

There's a cigarette tree by the beach.

The sun shines.

The cars on the road, they're going fast. And you, yes you, must remember to slow down.

My dear.

Do you remember the day we ran over a wagtail that was hopping about on the side of the road, it wasn't dead, it lay there on the roadside, and I had to reverse over the bird, we heard how the little body was crushed under the car wheels, and something between us died that day.

The sun was shining.
Thousands of people die on the roads each year.

Sylvia Plath committed suicide in the kitchen.

Isn't it a lovely day today.

The sky is cloudless and deep blue.

There's a car park by the beach.

From the air the cars look like hives. The bees fly in swarms and settle in the heather or in the clover field. We can't say that nature is good or bad.

The birds in the trees, they'll fly up. They'll fly up in a flock, a black cloud of birds.

The birds will be scared, but only for a moment, as after a gunshot, then they'll fly back to the trees, to their nests.

The birds, we can hardly see them, or the trees, each individual tree, neither the birch, nor the pine, nor the willow, nor the aspen whose leaves turn in the wind, nor the flowers by the side of the road and in the meadows, neither the dandelion, nor the butter-cup, nor the cress, nor the foxglove, nor the clover flower; you're driving too fast.

Now you're driving too fast again; I don't know if it's because you're unhappy or cross.

There's so much I wanted to say, so much I wanted to ask you about. We sit silently side by side in the car. I don't know you any more, after all these years.

If silence has a colour, it's blue.

The sun is shining.

We're driving into the light.

The colours will disappear. I've never loved anyone like I love you.

It Was Just a Thought, It Only Lasted a Moment

For a long time they couldn't decide where to live. She wanted to live in one part of the country, he in another. In the beginning it wasn't a big problem for them, she was from the east and he was from the west, and what had at first been an exotic difference—she'd grown up in a large detached house, he in a block of flats, she had a feeling for the forest and the flat, open landscape of the east, he was attached to the steep and enclosed valleys of the west—turned slowly, and almost imperceptibly, into an aloofness between them. A silence. They didn't talk about it, this aloofness, but it grew and bred more and more silence; the distance and the silence between them got bigger.

But when they were on holiday, or travelling, or when they were out driving, this aloofness was gone. When they drove the car, they were close. And when they drove fast, they were one: she loved speed, so did he.

He liked sitting in the passenger seat close beside her, watching her drive. She sat behind the wheel dressed in a blue shirt, jeans and leather boots, she changed gear and accelerated and talked quickly. She talked without inhibition when she drove. She turned her face towards him and often took her eyes off the road as she spoke. There was a savagery about her driving. Now, keep your eyes on the road, he might shout. You need to slow down, he might say. She spoke of the horses she'd ridden in her youth and about one of the horses which was bigger and wilder than the rest, and one day, when she was out riding this unruly horse, it got spooked by a car and left the road at full gallop, over the fields and through the forest and in an arc back to the road where she was terrified they'd be run over, she was sure she was going to die. He sat by her side and imagined her careering off on the big horse, out of control, at full gallop, riding between life and death. She went faster, following the edge of the road and the bends in the powerful, heavy car. The window was open on her side, her long hair blew like a tail at the back of her head, and sometimes it blew forwards into her face, over her eyes. He saw a dead fox on the carriageway. What if they hit an animal, an elk, a deer? He, she would be crushed against the steering wheel, against the dashboard. He suddenly felt a keen tenderness towards her and wanted to lean towards her and hold her and kiss her, and something in him didn't give a damn if they came off the road, if they crashed or died, if they couldn't live together, they could at least die together, it was just a thought, it only lasted a moment. He kissed her on the neck. She trod on the brake hard, slowed down, pulled in to the side of the road, stopped the car. Are you mad? she shouted. D'you want to kill us or something? I only wanted you to slow down, he lied. You drive too fast, he said. I drive just the same as you, she said. If I drive too fast, then you do too, but I don't go around kissing you while you're driving. I forbid you to touch me when I'm driving, don't even think of touching me again, don't touch me, d'you hear, ever, she said.

The Guest   For Merethe Lindstrøm

Today is his birthday. His fiftieth. He's put on his best suit and is celebrating the occasion alone.

The black velvet suit is tailor-made. A white, newly ironed shirt. Silver cufflinks. He smokes a cigarette.

He has a good dinner. Drinks an expensive wine. The living room is adorned with flowers, white lilies, a present to himself.

The lines in the lilies' leaves are like the veins beneath the skin of the hands holding the cutlery. He cuts his meat.

He takes a mouthful of wine. He looks at his hands, long and carefully, as if they are guests at the birthday celebration.

His hands remind him of the shadow pictures he made as a child, at night, in bed; all sorts of birds that flew from the wall and into his dreams.

The same fear that haunted him as a child remains with him as an adult; he is frightened of being alone.

He isn't alone. He's sitting here with his hands, with all these shadows that still come down from the walls.

The photograph of his mother. She's wearing an evening dress, low cut, her skin dark from the sun; she offers him a cigarette.

She's never permitted him to smoke with her; but today neither of them can gainsay that pleasure.

He's never dared tell her how fond he is of her, how beautiful he thinks she is.

Now he says it, and she gives him a smack on the hand. He pushes the hand into the right pocket of his jacket.

It's my birthday, he says. I know that, she says. Why are you alone? she asks.

You with your good looks and decent income, whose work is known and admired, and with a lovely house you've inherited, why are you alone?

He gets up and goes to the kitchen. Puts the coffee on. He likes his coffee-maker. He's fond of his lamps, his curtains, his furniture, a comfy chair.

He sits in the chair now on his return from the kitchen. Sometimes he thinks that he's as fond of objects as he is of people.

Perhaps that's your fault, he replies. My fault? she says. How can it be my fault that you're alone?

He's a man who cries. It often amazes him; that he cries so easily.

He drinks some coffee. Eats a piece of birthday cake. The first glass of spirits.

Darkness has begun to fall outside. It's growing dark, but he doesn't want to switch on the lamps.

He enjoys sitting in the living room watching the dusk gathering slowly. He likes sitting in the dark.

He liked hiding as a child. You liked hiding as a child, she says.

You hid behind doors and in cupboards, she says. He remembers it well: the exhilarating thrill of vanishing.

He hid behind doors and in cupboards. She had to look for him. He trembled with excitement, behind the door, in the cupboard, held his breath, stood stock still, he was waiting for her anguish.

He had gone. Disappeared. It was the only way to be loved.

You were a demanding child, she says, always said. You were quite impossible as a teenager and things only got worse over the years.

As an adult you were thoroughly headstrong and a most difficult person.

You've always gone your own way, never listened to advice, always done the opposite or something completely different to what you've been told.

It's your own fault you're alone, she says. It's my own fault I'm alone, he thinks.

I've turned into a difficult person, just like my mother; I'm becoming more and more like her.

The same obstinacy, the same need to rebel, the same desire for freedom, the same loneliness.

My mother's loneliness. He lights another cigarette. He holds the cigarette in his left hand between his middle and index fingers, waves the cigarette in an arc; a gesture of love. The embracing of himself.

I miss you, he says, out loud, in the empty living room. She's not answering any more, and suddenly he has the childish urge to do something forbidden on his birthday. He leaves the living room and walks up the stairs to the bedrooms and wardrobes on the first floor where nothing has changed since his parents lived here. He opens the door of the big wardrobe, pushes in-between his mother's dresses and sits down on the floor in the cupboard, pulls his knees up to his chin, his face between his legs, holds his breath and feels the quivering excitement, it washes over him, he's about to disappear, and just at that moment he's happy.

The Writer Who Doesn't Write

For Szilvia Molnar

Harold Costello lives in a seventeenth-century farmhouse, a short distance from Asolo, up the stone steps out of the village and through the forest, over a ridge and down a wooded hillside towards the unmetalled road that bends past a couple of dwellings before you spot the Costello house. A small gateway. A hawthorn hedge he must have planted after reading Proust. And yes: a bell fixed to the gate.

I took the train from Bergen to Oslo, then on to Copenhagen and straight down through Germany into Italy. Continuing by bus from Treviso to Asolo, two buses, you change to a smaller bus when the road narrows and climbs the mountainside towards the upland village. The passengers were disgorged by the fountain in the square. Close by there's a cafe with a terrace. I went there and made enquiries about Harold Costello but no one had heard of him. They didn't know him in the shops either, they didn't know who he was or where he lived. Didn't he live here? Was the man I'd met on a train journey in Austria a con man, wasn't he an American author who lived in Italy? And the books he'd said he'd written, perhaps they were written by another Costello, the right Costello, and he didn't live here, in Asolo. From the hairdresser I learnt that there was an American living a little distance from the village, the route lay through the forest, it was a forty-minute walk. At the grocer's I bought a piece of Parmesan, two bottles of red wine, a bottle of grappa, butter and bread. Then I set out through the forest.

It was late afternoon by now, nearly evening, nearly dark.

Harold didn't know I wanted to come, that I was on my way, nearly there.

The path wound twisting and narrow through the forest, rising at first, through smaller trees, then where it levelled out the trees were bigger; oaks and chestnuts with thick foliage that made the path murky and hard to follow. I came to a ridge and now the evening had turned dark. I wasn't sure which way to descend. The path divided, I had to make a decision. I sat down on a boulder to rest. Then I saw something I'd never experienced before: fireflies. They arrived in a swarm and, for a while, circled or danced, that's what it seemed like, above the rock I sat on. They were extraordinarily beautiful. Beautiful and frightening—these insects or flies that gleamed, that flew nearer and nearer my face and eyes, they hummed and shone in the dark, and I was encircled and dazzled by lights, by glowing insects that flew and imprisoned me in a small sphere of brightness; it was impossible to see anything in the darkness beyond. Gradually, the swarm moved away and, gripped by panic, I followed the direction the fireflies took. After some minutes, perhaps a quarter of an hour, I was at Harold Costello's house.

Harold sat in his garden in the dark reading by the light of a paraffin lamp. Was that him? I found the gate and pushed it open, the little bell that was fixed to it tinkled. He shouted something and rose from his garden chair. A tall figure, short, grey hair, a thin face, glasses; a refined, handsome, elderly man, just as I recalled him.

Harold, I said.

Who are you? he asked.

In the morning I found a cut rose in a vase on my bedside table. A biography of Proust lay on the bed by my pillow. Harold had been in my room during the night; I awoke with the feeling that he'd been in the room a long time.

My new room was large and bright with white-washed walls. A window with shutters. A writing table, lamp and chair. A door that opened on to a patio, roofed by the boughs of two rose bushes. The room resembled a monk's cell, there was a crucifix over the bed. I awoke and heard Harold outside the house, he was working in the garden.

I stood at the window and saw him clipping the hedge and tending the flowers, he raked leaves and gathered twigs into a pile, and I noticed that there was something feminine about the way he worked, in his movements and hands; the way he articulated his hands and wiped them on the apron he'd tied around his waist. As soon as he saw me at the window, he shouted that breakfast was ready in the kitchen.

He'd spread a yellow tablecloth on the kitchen table. It was laid with china plates and matching cups. Glasses and silver knives. Flowers in a vase. He'd baked bread and boiled eggs; we ate them with butter and drank freshly filtered coffee.

Ah, Harold, this must be the perfect place to write, I said. The house and the tranquillity, the beautiful rooms and the views of the forest. The narrow path leading to the village which is just far enough away.

He smiled. Rubbed his thumb up and down his nostril.

I worked on a book about Queen Kristina of Sweden for a long time but gave it up and began a book about Descartes which I was never happy with. I've attempted to write a novel, and for a time I wrote short stories. I've written poetry. I've written essays, but none of it got finished, and I haven't delivered a thing. I write every day. In Asolo, I'm known as the writer who doesn't write. That's because they've never seen a book with my name on it. I haven't had a book published since 1979 when I wrote *Miss Teste*. As you know, the novel was an international success. I made a bit of money, travelled around Europe and stumbled on this house which I bought. I thought that this would be the perfect place too, the perfect house, the perfect place to write. I moved here to write. Everything in the house and in the garden and all around me was arranged with just one object, to write. But in all the years I've lived here, I've never managed to write anything worthwhile. It's been my curse that I can't write the way I want to write, that I can't manage it here in these surroundings which are unsurpassed for an author, he said and turned thoughtful and quiet. D'you have your writing things with you? he asked, suddenly enthusiastic, as if he'd hit on some cunning chess move. I suggest that you stay on here just as long as you want. It'll be interesting for me to see if you manage to work here, and if what you write is bad, good or maybe just so-so. Is it a deal? he asked.

The very next day I moved a small wooden table on to the patio, in the shade beneath the rose bushes. I now had two writing tables, one by the window in my bedroom and one on the patio with a view of the garden and out towards the forest where every once in a while birds flew up. I could see deer and hares and small animals on the brow of the forest, and occasionally men and women on the path to and from Asolo. It was September. The sky was an untroubled blue. I was glad the few times it turned overcast, because the clouds afforded me a bit of distraction, and the rain, the rain was an event. It rained. The rain beat down. The shower lasted a few minutes, then the flowers and trees dripped. After the rain a fresh wind blew on to the patio, it was almost like having a visitor; I lit a cigarette and pushed the hair out of my face.

One day Harold asked if he could cut my hair. It was long and tied in a ponytail. I was proud of my long hair but I let him cut it. I sat on a stool in the garden. Harold got out scissors and a comb and cut my hair, first in big tufts, then clipped it really short at the sides and back. Harold held up a mirror and I saw that now I had the same hairstyle as him. In the evening—he'd cooked a special dinner—he asked if I wanted to borrow one of his old suits. I tried three different ones, chose a blue suit made of a thick felt-like material, single-breasted, with roomy trousers. He gave me a white shirt. A pair of clean cotton socks. We both sat, newly washed and shaved, at the table in the kitchen; Harold wanted to know how my writing was going. We had stock dove with chestnuts and mushrooms which he'd gathered. New potatoes from the garden. A bottle of local red wine. Birch and twigs were burning in the grate, they made such a homely, warm crackling from the kitchen hearth.

Have you been able to write as usual? Harold asked.

I'm writing every day, I said.

Have you formed any opinion about whether you're writing better or worse than normal, than you do at home? Well, you know what I'm driving at, have you noticed if this house and this place have any effect on what you write?

Hard to judge. It's too early to say, I haven't written that much, it's taking longer than normal, perhaps because it's so quiet here, I said, and not a lot happens either. I'm trying to describe the garden and the house, this place, I'm trying to describe the countryside.

I see, he said. Are you succeeding?

I don't know, I said. Perhaps I'll try writing about something completely different.

I see, he repeated, as if acknowledging the prob-lems of his entire adult life, of all the years he'd lived in the house without writing, because he no longer wrote, I'd realized that, although he sat at his writing table every day, for a few hours. He sat at the table and read, or stared out of the window, it was a terrible sight, an author inert and helpless at his desk, every day, without writing, he wrote nothing; he was the writer who didn't write.

But I am writing, I said, it may very well work. I've written the opening of a short story.

I see, he said listlessly, he hadn't anticipated that I'd be able to write anything in the house or on the patio. Has your story got a title? he enquired.

Yes, it has, I said. The story is called 'The Perfect Room'.

After a fortnight in Harold's house I'd written the beginning of a short story. It was slow work and gradually my writing ground to a halt. I sat in my room, or on the patio, and was unable to write. But I remained on the patio, morning and evening; I sat at the small wooden table and stared out at the forest or into the darkness which fell so fast and thickly at night. The sky turned starry and, when a full moon lit up the valley in which we lived, the house and the twilit garden were so bewitching and magic that I imagined that anything could happen here, in the garden, in the house, but nothing happened. Harold made no advances or overtures, even though I realized he was in love. I knew he came into my room while I slept, there were always fresh-cut flowers on my bedside table in the morning. We ate breakfast together and often took long walks in the hills around Asolo. We discussed literature and music. Harold was well read and intelligent, everything he said was interesting and original, it was hard to understand why he couldn't write. Occasionally, we took the path to Asolo where we sat on the cafe terrace and drank wine and smoked. People almost certainly regarded us as a couple—I was dressed in Harold's old suits, and maybe we looked alike, the younger and the older man spending their days and evenings in idleness and a kind of unencumbered happiness which, in reality, concealed a deep resignation and despair.

The Perfect Room   For Åshild Kanstad Johnsen

For many years, I lived in cheap flats and dingy rooms. Some of these rooms were so awful that I got rashes on my face and body, other rooms gave me chest problems and insomnia. But I wrote and worked steadily and regularly, unhindered and undisturbed by my many moves; I shifted from one depressing place to another, but could write anywhere and at any time, or so it seemed. Then one day I got a message that my sister was going to move out of her flat in Dreggen. I'd borrowed the flat from her several times, when she was travelling or on holiday; I was very fond of camping in the flat among her possessions and furniture. In many ways it was the perfect flat—it was in the city centre and had a view of the harbour, a bright, modern flat in a quiet district of the city, close to the church of Mariakirken. A large living room, kitchen, one bedroom and a bathroom. Now I had the chance to take the flat over. For the first time in my adult life, I'd be well housed, for as long as I wanted; in many ways, I was saved.

My sister moved out. I took up the carpets in the living room and bedroom, ripped and tore them up and laid new laminated wooden floors, a light wood, birch. I painted the living-room walls white, broken by a light shade of grey on the partitions. The kitchen light green, a mint colour. The bedroom blue, a deep blue tint. I bought a new, firm double bed. Bookshelves. A leather sofa. And best of all: a wide, long writing table that took up the whole of one wall. A desk lamp, also of wood, with a metal shade, its light was ideal. The living room I'd furnished was just right.

I was in the process of creating the perfect room. I developed it slowly; bought the necessary books, a new reading light, a good chair. I threw away surplus things, replaced them with utilitarian objects, a knife, an ashtray, a teacup. With the money I earned from my novel *Biography* (*Oblivion*), I bought bowls,

candlesticks, ashtrays, pencils, knives, curtains, cush-
ions, bedclothes, lamps, a couple of radios and some
pornographic prints.

Whenever I took the lift up to the top floor and
opened the door to my penthouse and walked into
the hall from where I could see into the living room,
I was always filled, each time I did it, with deep contentment and pure joy. I'd never seen a more beautiful living room. I stayed in the flat for two years.
During the two years I lived in that flat in Dreggen,
I never managed to write a single novel, not so much
as a short story.

Bergeners   For Cecilie Løveid

Erlend O. Nødtvedt smokes like an athlete. He's
dressed in a white shirt, a light-brown cashmere
sweater, the jacket of a green-check suit and light
trousers. Good shoes. At night, he plays pieces
he's composed himself on a pump organ which he
got from Yngve Pedersen. During the day, he writes
poetry. In a small one-roomed flat in Lodin Leppsgate,
he writes poetry that is bigger than the city he lives
in but maybe not as big as the room he inhabits. It's
a shabby room: a writing table, chair, bed, surrounded by bookshelves and books, a pump organ,
that's all. That's all he needs to live. He sits at his

writing table. We drink wine and smoke. He smokes cigarettes like a woman. He's dressed in a light-blue blouse that's open at the neck. His hair is cut short at the sides and back, it hangs in a long, red mop over his forehead. That pale forehead. That pale face, that pale skin—he's almost transparent, but it's because the darkness within him hasn't yet turned black. He's young. He can be silent. He smokes a pipe like an old man. Old before his time, he wants to be young. He's disguised as a young man in a black shirt and black trousers. Black shoes. He smokes like a demon.

First a sniff of wind, and then the wind comes, damp and cold, it's a fresh, good wind. The wind comes like a good, much-needed breath from another place. The wind comes from the sea. The wind comes from the sun, from the clouds, from the mountains, from west or north, the wind comes like a harbinger. Here comes the wind. It touches the hair and face. It pulls at jackets and trousers and pushes us along the city streets. The wind comes like a harbinger of rain.

It'll be raining soon, it's raining now, rain falls. That hard, gentle rain. Tentatively at first, filmy. Small flowers of water. In the air. With the wind, water flowers in the air, with the wind. The way the water droplets unfurl and burst open in the air. The way the water droplets form themselves into a more powerful stream, a harder fall, a heavier rain. It beats. The rain beats against the head and throat.

The rain whips and beats, against the throat and mouth, against the windows and doors, against the roofs and walls, against the eyes and face. Hard water. Heavy water, it's no longer rain but water that falls. A grey, malevolent water that falls.

All this water, it feels like home. Like living in a grey, wet darkness, it doesn't vanish. A strip of light. A clearing in the air. A shimmer, which cuts and divides the horizon, sky and sea. And above the sea that rises and the water that falls, a gathering of clouds. White, grey, black clouds being woven into one another, masses and threads, they weave a web in the sky, a heavenly and lovely web of clouds that changes and changes with the wind. Now the water is falling. Now we're home.

A noteworthy figure in the rain, tall, like a wading bird; he walks with long strides and a slight weakness in his left leg. Walking stick, thick pince-nez, a high-crowned hat. Were you, for any reason, forced to disturb him, shake his hand, he'd introduce himself as Herr Joyce. He speaks pidgin Norwegian, short, intelligent sentences. He doesn't say much. He's put up at Sontums Hotel, on the corner of Nordnesgate and Tollbodallmenning; Ibsen stayed there too, he says.

They build and demolish. The city undergoes constant change, it remains unchanged. They could tear down the whole city and rebuild it, a new city, and the inhabitants of the new city wouldn't have altered one jot. The same language, the same arrogance, the same hankering for argument and trouble. The same proclivity to reproduce and throw strangers out of town. The same cloddish interest in trade and money. The same old eagerness for building and demolishing, despite the fact that no alteration has ever altered the slightest thing about the city.

Georg Johannesen stands in the rain at the entrance to the Faculty of Arts on Nygårdshøyden, wearing a red knitted jumper, green corduroy trousers, gumboots, surrounded by a group of new-intake students.

D'you lot know why Bergeners are so much stupider than other Norwegians? he asks.

We shake our heads, tramp our feet, jerk our arms. We await the oracle's reply.

Because they're always holding umbrellas and all the blood that should circulate round their heads pumps out to their right hands, Georg Johannesen says.

Why is it, the woman with the soaked face says, her mouth is wet, she spits out the words, they land on my face like water; it's impossible to tell if she's crying or if her eyes are full of rain; why is it we put up with living in this city, year after year, it's making me ill, living in this dampness, summer and winter, autumn and spring. I want to walk down the street in light clothes, wearing my blouses, dry shod, with unencumbered hands, a handbag, bare-headed; that's impossible without being humiliated by this wetness that rains down on us all the time.

Can a city ruin a love affair?

She comes from Oslo, he's from Bergen, it's like being two lovers who are worlds apart, like the ones Shakespeare described. It's almost as if she's a Capulet and he a Montague. Janne, he says one evening as they sit on her balcony in Michael Krohnsgate: Let's move to Copenhagen.

Suddenly the sun pierces the layer of cloud which breaks up and moves slowly eastwards. The sky clears. Soon it's an unbroken blue. A blue vault of sky that lights up the city and its streets; it's spring. Clear, sharp spring air rises from the cobbled streets and seeps out of the trees on the mountainside where the snow is melting and the streams gush in great waterfalls down the slopes before flowing out and flooding the city.

It shames Bergeners that none of them have a good word to say about the capital, about Oslo, Norway's second most important city. Whenever I meet Ole Robert Sunde in Bergen, he always says, Bergen's a lovely city, it never rains when I'm here. This is the rhetoric of the capital; you praise the periphery, the landscape and architecture, the weather and literary culture of the smaller cities. The Bergener puffs himself up by commenting disparagingly on the capital. When the Bergener speaks of Oslo, Bergen swells; the city becomes greater and greater and terribly important before it vanishes completely in mist and rain.

Early one Saturday afternoon in August 2011, Henning H. Bergsvåg and I walked through the city dressed in our best clothes. We were going to a party at Cesilie Holck and Olav Øyehaug's. The party was in Torborg Nedreaasgate, in the flat where we'd had some of our best parties. We went with high expectations each carrying a rucksack on our back. Henning in a dark suit, mauve shirt, black shoes. A black, narrow-crowned hat, he swung his arms like a young, elderly man. Cloudless sky. Trees in full leaf. The church bells of Johanneskirken struck two; we walked side by side as friends do, each involved in the other, arms and legs. That poem, Henning, I asked, where Kristian Lundberg and Håkan Sandell walk through the streets of Malmö together, do you remember it? Everything is so exact in that poem: the streets, the addresses, the names, the houses, the clouds, the temperature, the date, the conversations. There's no poetry in the poem, no device and metaphor, only description and realism, that's how we must write, I said, and we turned a street corner, walked straight on along Vaskerelven. Henning didn't reply, and when I looked to the left to make sure he hadn't managed to loosen the ties that bound us so tightly together, I noticed that a thin, fair, shoulder-length hair had sprouted from under his black hat. We must describe the city we live in, the times we live in, our friends, our discussions, our politics, our loneliness. We mustn't lose ourselves in a made-up, hypothetical universe, a false literature; what we write must be true, and we must describe what's real with all we possess of earnestness and strength, I said. I noticed now how his new flaxen hair was turning darker. It changed colour and curled into long locks that hung down on either side of his face, which turned thinner, sterner. A bushy beard sprouted around his mouth. His beard got thicker and longer as we walked. His clothes, too, were changing: a long, black, dress-like tunic covered him as he progressed, it hung beneath a loose-fitting, dark overcoat. His hat shrank and altered shape, it resembled a skullcap. Henning, I said, We must preserve reality by imitating it. We crossed Ole Bullsplass. In Valkendorfsgate, we bought three bottles of wine, spirits and some bottles of English beer which we divided between the rucksacks. Then we headed towards Verftet for dinner. The sun was shining. We sat outside, on the quay, with a view of the fjord and the shipyard cranes on Laksevåg. People were still bathing in the sea, diving from the quay, boys and girls; it was the perfect day.

The black, heavy garments fell from Henning like a slough of superfluous skin. He lost his hair and beard. His hair loosened from his scalp. His beard fell from his cheeks. He was bald and smooth of face, his hair lay in tufts on the dark heap of clothes which looked like an animal on the ground. Henning wanted to bathe. He wanted to swim in the sea. It wasn't hard to imagine him leaping off the quay and mutating in the air. What did he want to be most of all, a bird, a fish or another animal? He jumped into the sea but nothing happened. He just disappeared below the surface and emerged at the water's edge as the old, the true Henning.

We walked back into the city centre again. Bought flowers for Cesilie and Olav in Kong Oscars-gate. Henning delivered his hat for sprucing up and un-denting in Hollendergaten. I had new buttons sewn on to the jacket of my suit by an African tailor in Nikolaikirkeallmenningen. We were on our way to Øvregaten to fetch Erlend. Now there were three of us. Have you heard that Cecilie Løveid has moved back into town? Yes, we had heard. We'd got to pick up Magnus and Espen. We'd got to pick up Mari and Mari. We were going to meet Hildegunn. Now there were eight of us. We had to collect Henning's hat. We walked in a crowd over Nygårdshøyden. We were going to meet Kristina and her friends. Now we were eleven, no ten, no twelve. We walked in the direction of Nobel Bopel on Møhlenpris to meet Yngve and Øyvind. Carina and Trude-Kristin were sitting there, now we were sixteen. Maybe seventeen, maybe more. When's the party starting? It's begun. Is Mazdak coming, is Sigurd coming, is Susanne coming, is Audun coming? Is Bernhard coming, is Frode coming, are Eivind and Elisabeth coming, Jan Roar and Charlotte? Yes, they're coming, we're coming, we're on our way, in Welhavensgate, we're coming now. A good poem, Henning said, has no rules, a good party lasts till nine in the morning.

For a time, during the nineties, I visited Erling Aadland every Friday in his office for coffee and a smoke. His office lay at the heart of a labyrinth. You pulled the end of a ball of red wool behind you, mounted and descended stairs, went round and round corridors, knocking on various doors, until you finally heard, from the semi-darkness that hid and partially camouflaged him, his answering voice, a grey-clad man in a grey dawn: Come in, he'd say.

His office was beautiful in an uncomfortable way. It was the discomfort you feel in a smoke-filled room overladen with books; the books stood or lay on two racks on either side of the desk which was itself weighed down with papers and books. Books lay in piles on the floor and covered the two chairs that were reserved for guests. Nothing about the room indicated that you were wanted here, on the contrary, you had to force your way in, clear a space for yourself. In one corner, behind the door, stood a woman in uniform. She had a military cap pulled down over her eyes, a brown, soldier's uniform with shiny buttons, a cigarette in her hand. Erling sat at the desk, under the desk lamp. The office had a window with a view of Løvstakken and the city's fjord, but the curtains were drawn. Our regular meeting began, as always, with him giving me half his packed lunch, two slices of bread and cheese. He poured coffee from a thermos, into two cups, rolled two cigarettes, we smoked. I asked him what he was reading. He was reading Heidegger. After reading Hegel for a long time, for several years, he was now reading Heidegger, and I asked him if he'd embarked on an alphabet of the history of philosophy. Don't pretend to be stupid, he said; I'm not reading chronologically or at random. It was around this time that he started to become hard of hearing, a handicap he exploited in many ways; each time I said something he didn't like, and that was often, he would simply remark: I can't hear what you're saying. I said that Heidegger wrote badly, dreadful German, an inflated, nauseating style, almost unreadable, and physically repugnant. He heard me that time. We didn't agree about anything, nothing at all, perhaps that was why we liked each other. Every Friday we fought the same battle. He was a tricky opponent, half man, half bull. A broad face, keen, powerful eyes and thick, sensuous lips. He was coarsely made and elegant, refined in a bestial manner, as if he belonged to nature rather than the culture that had spawned him, and which he disliked. It was always possible to predict what he'd say, but he always said it in new ways, more polished and better formulated ways, and sometimes in cruder and more vulgar ways, he was master of the oath and foul language. He said, You know as well as I do that the most important literature has already been written. I'd riled him by what I'd said about Heidegger, now he wanted to get his own back, and this blow was designed to do extra damage because he knew I was trying to write novels. We have Hamsun's books, he said. We have Ibsen's plays. We have Wergeland's poems. We have Skram's novels, none of today's writers come anywhere near Skram, and she isn't one of our most powerful. Despite this, contemporary authors go on shamelessly penning a mountain of books, one book after the other, so why do they do it, he demanded, but it wasn't a question. I'd been hit but not shaken. I was used to these tirades and parried them as best I could. We went several rounds in his office. He fought rather like Joe Frazier, a tight, compact defence and quick attack, he threw short, hard punches. When we were both exhausted and marked, when we were both satisfied, we came together somewhere about the middle of the floor and shook hands. The battle was over. I followed the red skein out of the office and along the corridors, up and down stairs and out of the labyrinth that was the Department of General and Comparative Literature, out of the main entrance, through the glass door and out into the sunshine, out into the cold, fresh spring air.

A man walks up and down, on exactly the same beat, every day, wearing the same clothes, with a small pack on his back, to and fro, a circumscribed stretch, along Nygårdsgaten. He walks up from Danmarksplass every morning at nine, and doesn't leave his beat until four o'clock. It's a disquieting sight. It's almost as if this particular section of Nygårdsgaten is becoming less and less frequented. It's as if he empties the street; you can't bear to look at him, every single day, walking up and down. At first you probably feel sorry for the man, walking back and forth seems so pointless, to spend so much time doing the same thing every day. But gradually, as the days and weeks and months pass, maybe we start thinking of what we spend our own time doing, and when we meet him for the seventh or eighth time, it strikes some of us that our existence is as petty and meaningless as his, that our days are repetitive and dull, encompassing a larger area of the city, certainly, but from then on we avoid that particular stretch of Nygårdsgaten.

For a time, Lasse Myrvold lived with his girl-friend right in the heart of the city, in Vaskerelven. At weekends they were troubled by noise from the nightspots, from drunks yelling in the streets. Lasse got to sleep in the evenings without difficulty, something that irritated his girlfriend lying there sleepless. She lay awake listening to the dreadful racket in the streets. In despair, she roused Lasse: How can you possibly sleep? she asked. Well, can't you hear, he said, it's the sound of animals. I pretend we're living in the country and that we're surrounded by horses and dogs and cows and sheep, and then I drop off to sleep, Lasse said.

Hildegunn Dale goes canoeing and rock climbing in the mountains. She takes long walks with a wolfhound. Once, when I was teaching her to box, late one night, at a party, we were skipping round the living room, she loosed off, at only her third attempt, a perfect punch. Her right arm shot out from the shoulder in a straight line so quickly and powerfully that it was impossible to stop the clenched fist, it scored a direct hit and split my lip. That's probably one of my dearest possessions, the Hildegunn-scar on my upper lip. When she's had a drink or two, she frequently gets the urge to climb out of the window or down from the third-floor balcony where we're sitting smoking. She'll lean out and assess the facade, the places where she can lower herself and find footholds, ledges she can reach and grasp. Don't do it, Hildegunn, I say. You're not immortal yet. You'll have to write two or three more anthologies yet.

Kristian Linz complains that life is too good. We're walking through the city, into Olav Kyrresgate, then right on to Håkonsgate, left on to Vestre Torggate and up the hill and steps towards the church of Johanneskirken. The sun is shining, it's cold. Kristian is a good-looking young man, the girls turn to look at him; he's wearing a battered hat, a sheepskin jacket and Spanish boots made of Spanish leather. He carries his guitar in a case on his back. He's got a girlfriend, they've just bought a flat together. He's got a black sports car, a job he enjoys, he's content, he's in a good mood, he's happy. Life is good, so he's unable to write songs, he says. He's got a good band. He's got six good songs. But six songs aren't enough for an album, not enough to do concerts; everyone knows he's young and promising, everyone expects great things of him. But he can't write even one new song, and that's the way it's been for some years; time is passing, his hair is receding, his youth is vanishing like an impatient dog, soon it'll be time to think about children. Happiness is about to ruin my career, he says, I just can't write good songs when my life is good.

Frode Helmich Pedersen gives a talk on metamorphosis in Ulvik. In the evening, at his hotel, Room 101, with its little patio that has a view of an apple tree, Erlend, Henning, Kristina, Frode and I all discuss Ovid. Should one call him Ovid or Ovidius? If

you say Ovidius, you're indicating that you're familiar with Latin. If you say Ovid, it could mean that
you're familiar with Norwegian, Frode says before
taking off his glasses and turning into a wolf.

Cesilie Holck is the wildest and maddest and most
beautiful of us all. She used to be one, and then she
became two, now soon to be three.

The Aadland brothers are so unalike that they resemble each other.

What's become of the Aadland brothers anyway, you
never see them now, Frode says. We're driving
through Hardanger, like some slightly offbeat family,
none of us is sober, Erlend is driving. Øyvind has
taken up tennis, Vemund has got a girlfriend and
Yngve Pedersen's playing poker—they've all been
consumed by their own form of gaming folly, Erlend
says, driving into a tunnel much too fast.

Richard Aarø relates that he and Selma were on a
car trip in Italy with the kids. In St Peter's Square,
Rome, they chanced upon another family from
Bergen who were touring Italy by car. Which route
did you take to get down here? Richard asked in his
broadest Bergen dialect. We took the Kvamskogen
route, the other driver replied.

When I made my debut with Gyldendal and visited
the publisher's in Oslo for the first time, I was sum-
moned to Brikt Jensen's office. He'd heard I came
from Bergen. I walked up the stairs and probed my
way through the warren that hid the great office
which had once belonged to Harald Grieg. Brikt
Jensen sat behind a desk overflowing with books and
manuscripts, he was reputed to read three books a
day. He motioned me to sit in a chair. I hear you're
from Bergen and that you live in Bergen, he said in a
thick Bergen accent. Well, I've got something important to tell you, so listen carefully: Move away from
Bergen. If not, you'll become a Bergener, he said. If
you stay in Bergen, you'll become like Arild Haaland
or Georg Johannesen, Brikt Jensen announced, suddenly aroused and bellowing; he thumped his hand
repeatedly on the desk to emphasize the importance
of his words and I couldn't help thinking that
moving away and spending more than half his life in
Oslo hadn't done an awful lot for him.

Pål Norheim has sought sanctuary in a basement in
Eidsvåg. He lives there. Only four or five of us know
this. He's written three very good books, more people know that, but not all that many. Pål is hardly a
secretive person, and yet we don't know a lot about
him. He talks to few people, but those he does talk
to, he talks to for hours, often for days; on the odd
occasions when I meet him, always in the evening, at
a literary do—he'll arrive suddenly, startlingly, just

like the unexpected rare glimpse of an eagle, or a fox, or an elk; his stately, thin figure picking its way through the venue, light-footed, silent, as if walking through a forest, alert, with a beer glass in his hand, an unlit cigarette between his fingers—he's dressed and equipped to listen and discuss for hours, for days and nights. We start the conversation immediately after the reading is over and sit round the table until last orders. The four or five of us left take a taxi back to my place. We talk the whole night. Pål says that he belongs to the lumpenproletariat, and there is something aristocratic in the way he says this, the way he speaks, the way he rolls tobacco, the way he smokes, the way he drinks, the way he uses his hands, the way he sits on the sofa, so upright, so elegant, the way he squeezes one eye shut and opens the other wide when he becomes enthusiastic or angry. Of all of us, he's the most interesting and rewarding to listen to. He has, in common with Monsieur Teste, 'visited a few countries, dabbled in life's affairs without becoming too involved in them, eaten nearly every day and meddled with women'. We talk until daybreak. When it gets light, when the day begins, some of us sleep on mattresses or in beds. Pål lies on the living-room sofa smoking. When I wake up later in the morning, he's lying on the sofa reading. I make breakfast and filter coffee. My guests come to and we resume the conversation where we left off, with Ernst Jünger or H. C. Andersen. Thomas Boberg does a superb retelling of *The Shadow*. We discuss

Heidegger and Celan, open a wine-box and sit around in the living room all day, go out on the patio in the evening, smoke and drink shots. There's nothing we don't talk about. There's a crescent moon and the sky is starry. The first snow has settled on the tops of Lyderhorn and Damsgårdsfjellet. My guests are tired and want to go home or to bed, but Pål and I sit on at the coffee table in the living room, we stay there all night, until a new day dawns and Pål suddenly gets up from the sofa, puts on his coat and lights a cigarette, goes out of the door, turns and glances back into the living room, it's the glance of a man who's setting out on a long journey, or who'll be away some time: Well, it's time I got back to work, he says.

Cecilie Løveid settles herself in the black taxi, in the back seat, her red hair loses its colour as the courtesy light in the taxi fades, goes out. It's night. The city's lights don't make any impact on the car's windows, they glide over the glass, as if the car is standing still and the city is slipping past, sinking. It's raining. The hard raindrops beat on the car roof, a soothing patter, a kind of music: Do you remember that piano piece by Franz Liszt that describes weeping? Cecilie closes her eyes, she wants to sleep in the car. She'd like to wake up in another town or in an unknown place where her house stands white and tall in a garden, or is it a forest? Why can't you drive me to a house that isn't my own? The driver, a young man, is he Iranian, grasps the steering wheel so confidently and gently, is he sleeping? Yes, he's asleep. Perhaps he's dreaming of his town, his street, his house, his mother, sister, brother, of everything he's left behind; we're both so far from home, Cecilie mutters softly as the car drives past the house where she lives.

Åshild Kanstad Johnsen's studio is at Bergen Kjøtt, the old slaughterhouse in the Bontelabo cold-storage building, she shares a large, bright, grey room on the third floor with three other artists, they work during the day, she works at night. Her books and illustrations are light, the drawings she does for herself are dark, almost black. She sits alone in the darkened room, drawing by the light of a desk lamp. It's quiet in the room, in the whole of the great slaughterhouse where she can imagine the bellows of the animals being brought into the hall downstairs, before being electrically stunned and cut open in one long incision from their throats over their bellies and down to their genitals which are cut off and thrown into a red plastic tub on the bloody floor.

Silje Aa has left the city. The city hasn't realized it, like some earthquake no one notices, but for a short period the ground really did tremble, a few house walls shook, one drinking glass chinked against another, a knife tipped off the edge of the table and fell to the floor, a man banged his head on the kitchen table with all his strength.

Linda Maria lives right opposite; I can see my shadow in her living room in the evenings. All the rooms in her house are white, white walls, like great film screens, or fabric mesh in a Chinese shadow theatre. White light from white lamps. Linda is tall and dark, she has a deep, dark laughter: You see, it's not that I like living alone, but my height and appearance scare off the men I want, she laughs. Her shadow is alarmingly long with legs like crutches and an upper body that stretches across the living room furniture. The shadow runs up the walls, right up to the ceiling where her slender throat and angular profile fly across its vault as if the shadow is locked up in a cage and is searching for a nook or cranny in the ceiling through which to escape.

Øyvind Rimbereid is an incomer. He rides his bike on the wrong side of the road. He cycles straight ahead, following an invisible, straight line of his own. Then he brakes and stops, dismounts and staggers so wildly that you can't fail to be impressed at how straight he rides when he's drunk. If you'd kept going straight ahead, at that speed, Øyvind, I say, you'd have been a dead author. He regards me with the furious, scornful look of the fearless: Well you, you like writing of course, he says.

Simen Hagerup pays a visit. His hairstyle seems to indicate that he wants short hair and long hair at the same time.

Editor Lindholm lives at The Residence in Møhlenpris. Experiments are carried out in this flat, which is a laboratory, into consciousness-enhancing substances. LSD stands for Lindholm's Style Directives; and if you swallow them, you run the risk of writing tomorrow's books.

Marie, Marie, Maria and Embla practise in a flat in Møhlenpris, the music pounds out of the open window and the passer-by takes a couple of sidesteps before continuing.

The trees in Nygårdspark have lost their leaves and have spread autumn on the ground. A damp underlay woven in yellows and reds, it's like walking on a carpet out of doors.

Someone's shooting up under the trees. A man is lying on the ground. His face is white. The passer-by halts, a shout comes to him from the darkness beneath the trees: Leave Ola be, this is the third time he's taken an overdose, all he wants is to die.

A crow flies up, it's black and lighter black and ever lighter as it rises. The black crow is caught by the sunlight and flies away like a white crow in the park.

An elderly woman with a child, throwing pieces of bread to the pigeons. The pigeons settle on the child's head and shoulders and the little boy screams and suddenly gets feathers and wings.

And there, at the end of the park, just outside the gate—a monument by the artist Per Kirkeby. The monument is a basilica with colonnades and a church door which you go through to pee.

Perhaps your steps turn towards Danmarksplass. Jonas Rolsted wrote: My eyes rested here several times.

The Ballad of Danmarksplass, of Denmark, of the junction, of this place where Denmark isn't.

This is the intersection of Fjøsangerveien, Ibsensgate and Michael Krohnsgate.

One car smashes into another and two lovers die, everything you need for dying, is there in Danmarksplass.

There's a cemetery on the rise above Fjøsangerveien. There's a petrol station in Michael Krohnsgate.

There's an empty flat in Ibsensgate. Charlotte lived there once.

Oh Danmarksplass. With no Denmark. With no Charlotte, with no Josefine, with no Olga, with no Stine, with no Suzanne, with no

Pia, with no Mette, with no Amalie, with no Maja, with no Janne—what are you really doing here in these streets with no name?

With no city. Just a junction where cars meet in their own passing haste. Just streets, no city. No forest.

No trees. No fields or marshes. No wildlife. No river. Just this timeless stream of traffic that

pours that trickles that roars that snakes past. That flows in torrents past Nothingness-plass.

Danmarksplass. What does the passer-by do here, what is there to do here? Perhaps he loves this particular place which is never the same; nor is he ever the same in Danmarksplass, either.

All you need for dying is here in Danmarksplass. The cars whizz past at high speed.

The high-rise flats stand in rows and stretch into blocks; they throw shadows and gather

dust and exhaust in small, box-like back yards where the inhabitants can go and smoke. How beautiful they are, these

solarium-brown faces that are strangers to fresh air. These eyes that have no need of natural things.

What do we want with nature? We've managed perfectly well all our lives with hard work, with industry and rest.

We sleep with the windows shut. Some of us have double windows. Some of us have damaged ears, we can't hear

noise. The view of the factory buildings and shipyard cranes is the right one for a worker.

Some of us vote for the Progress Party. Everyone ought to be for progress, better roads, less tax.

Fewer Arabs in the country. Fewer Afghans, fewer Pakistanis, fewer Somalis, fewer Muslims in our country.

No foreigners in Danmarksplass! They don't work, and they haven't got cars, so what are they doing here?

We don't want any mosques, no calls to prayer, no Allah in Danmarksplass. There's no God in Danmarksplass.

No Jesus either.

Seen in the right way, there's a certain beauty about Danmarksplass. A certain emptiness. A certain silence.

Suburban silence at night as Danmarksplass shines, flares up and dies down, like northern lights and phosphorus and neon.

Yellow and red automobile blooms, they move in the wind, the traffic light poles sway in the darkness like steel trees.

With darkness come the colours: blue, green, red, yellow in sharp relief, a harder environment.

A metal plate suddenly illuminated by car headlights, a hard, rectangular second sun in the night.

You should drive through Danmarksplass at night. It's a place for cars, for lovers in cars,

a place for loneliness in cars. You drive. You aren't going anywhere. You drive fast.

Smoke a cigarette. Play music, kiss, you put your arms around each other in the car. Wouldn't it have been nice to be able

to fall asleep and wake up in the car. Wouldn't it have been nice to be able to make love in the car, at speed.

Wouldn't it have been nice to be able to die in the car. All you need for dying, is here in Danmarksplass.

There are three empty rooms in Michael Krohnsgate. A bright flat with a balcony and a view of the harbour.

The shipyard cranes, the docks and the engine hall where they built and repaired engines. The quay where they unloaded engine parts.

It's quiet in the harbour, in the shipyard, in the engine hall, on the quay, just as it's quiet in the flat.

She whose flat it was has left Michael Krohnsgate, but the passer-by takes the route

through Nygårdspark, across Danmarksplass and into long Michael Krohnsgate, every single day.

Each day he walks to the flat in Michael Krohnsgate, as he used to, as he did when she lived there.

Many people leave the city, move out. Many people can't stand living in Bergen too long; the freedom-robbing rain and the damp confinement between mountains leaves them ill and drained. You're forced to live indoors, alone or in small families. You walk from house to house, from premises to premises, from bar to bar, from inside to inside. You could empty the city of all its inhabitants and fill it up with entirely new people, but the city would remain the same.

There are people who never move, who stay and who, in many cases, live as close as possible to the place where they grew up. These are the people Dag Haugstvedt calls 'homies'; there is a note of pride in his statement, as if it's a mark of respect, or a matter of honour: You endure, you remain in your native city, in your district and street. Perhaps you've inherited your parents' house. Perhaps, like me, you live in the same room you had as a child.

Dag Haugstvedt lives in his grandparents' house. His son plays football for the same club he belonged to as a youth. Dag has many talents and produced an anthology of poems that was never published. I meet Dag at the artificial grass pitch at Stemmemyren, he's standing with his chums, they've never left the neighbourhood either and are now husbands and fathers and are happy in that difficult way; we watch the football, eat hot dogs and drink coffee out of paper cups.

The People of Hellemyr

Just below the football pitches at Stemmemyren, beyond the bend that turns into Helleveien, lies Hellen School. On our first day there, as seven-year-olds, when we had to line up, by classes, in the school playground shelter next to the signs with the classroom numbers written on them, I ended up, quite by chance, standing next to the girl who was to become my wife. My mother had made me a suit for the occasion—a single-breasted, brown tweed jacket and newly pressed matching trousers, a suit I wore in addition to a square leather satchel on my back, a light-coloured polo-necked sweater, brown leather shoes, all that was missing was a packet of cigarettes.

It's no exaggeration to say that I was surprised to discover that I was the only boy in my class, in fact, as far as I could see, in the entire school, who'd arrived for the first day of term at Hellen School in a suit. My father had already seen the head teacher, Fru Førde, and demanded that I was moved from the class in which I'd originally been placed, the so-called Skytterveien class, which was filled entirely with children from the street of residential blocks where I lived, Skytterveien. That class would wreck me, and my entire future, my father contended, and behind him, was my mother. So now I stood besuited in a class consisting of children from Eikeviken, and Biskopshavn and Solbakken and from all the posh addresses and families which had despatched their children to school in ordinary clothes. There were just two things for me to do at Hellen School: take off my heavy jacket and learn to fight.

I lived in a high-rise block in Skytterveien, but my friends and schoolmates were from the villas in Eikeviken and Biskopshavn. The houses down by the sea were light-filled and large, with lots of living room windows and open patio doors through which the scents of garden and sea wafted into the houses and billowed the pale curtains like a mild wind, a summer breeze through rooms of inherited furniture and thick carpets, piano in the living room, stairs to the bedrooms below and to the dining room above, bookshelves and artwork on the walls, countless lamps, what riches, what beauty in the houses by the sea. I couldn't possibly invite any of these children, who were my friends, from the houses here, back to my own home. And I never did, not once.

These children, who were my friends, weren't my friends. The only children who could visit me on the tenth floor of the high-rise block were children who lived on the third or fifth or ninth floor, in other words, children who lived in the same block. A child or a teenager from my own class could never go there, children with names like Vossgård, Sæverud, Brudvik, Teigland or Warncke, it was unthinkable. I've heard it put about, and it has been mentioned that certain authors in Oslo are suggesting that a writer from Bergen should come up with a novel about Bergen's middle classes. And I've been told that the said authors from Oslo think that the said writer from Bergen should be me. All right. A novel about Bergen's bourgeoisie, here goes: 'Ole Christian Mohn Lunde grew up in a detached house in Biskopshavn, Ytre Sandviken, by the sea. He did well at school, without too much effort, and his good marks and exemplary conduct gained him entrance to Bergen Cathedral School where he met Trine-Lise Egedius who hailed from Hop in Fana; for a number of years they squabbled about whether to set up house and start a family in Ytre Sandviken or Fana, but after the wedding they moved into one of the Egedius family's houses in Fana where they live a quiet and secluded life.'

Bergen's middle class is the most boring and unexciting phenomenon imaginable; what can you write about it, about them, about these almost invisible families, which are hardly ever seen or heard of, what is there to say? That one of them has changed his job, from one firm to another, that he's divorced, that he's met a younger woman, that he's moved back to Ytre Sandviken where he grew up?

In the area known as Hellen, which comprised a few small, unproductive farms and later also villas and detached houses with sea views, the early sixties saw the construction of a large number of residential blocks, at Lønborg, and at Fagernes, on Skytterveien and on Øyjordsveien. Then these quiet, beautiful seaside spots were inundated with families from every social class with kids and teenagers who immediately formed themselves into gangs and spent all their free time in banditry and street wars and gang showdowns. The area was turned into a battleground. On 23 April 1977, the gangs in Skytterveien mobilized a combined force and made ready to advance across

the hump of Øyjordfjellet, down the path known as
Olinestien, through Fagerdalen, the district once
known as Hellemyren, past the lake of Helvedesvan-
net and then straight ahead towards the residential
blocks of Lønborg, those neighbouring blocks, this
enemy territory that was to be taken, to annihilate
the gangs there, principally the Lønborg Angels who
were posing a threat to the bandits of Skytterveien.
Maybe a girl was involved, too. Practically a kidnap-
ping, as one of the Skytterveien girls had become the
sweetheart of the gang leader of the Lønborg Angels.
The army from Skytterveien numbered twenty-three,
boys equipped with air rifles, dogs, knives and sling-
shot, sticks and stones. They formed a column. The
biggest boys first, with dogs, the smallest in the
middle and a rear guard of brothers, there were the
Heldal brothers and the Wiers brothers and the
Jakobsen brothers. Then the advance across of the
mountain began. It was a Saturday, at 3 p.m. The
Battle of Hellemyren lasted all afternoon and minor
skirmishes continued into the evening, until it was
dark. The final encounter took place at Helleneset
where one of the Lønborg gangs had gathered round
a bonfire; that wasn't unusual at the weekends, boys
and girls sitting by the sea, round a fire, drinking
beer. Some of them were shot at with air rifles. Others were bitten by dogs. A couple were thrown into
the sea. Most were chased away, from Helleneset.
The bonfire was scattered and put out. It was pissed
on. The battle was over. The street war had been

won. In precisely a week's time, next Saturday, the whole thing would repeat itself, but in the opposite direction: the Lønborg gangs would gather to cross the mountain to Skytterveien.

The People of Hellemyr, as Amalie Skram had once immortalized them, the new people, were a mixture of children and teenagers from every stratum of society, sons and daughters of architects, watchmakers, opticians, electricians, industrial workers, seamen and social security clients; you didn't see the parents, they were out working. They were resting. They were doing their own thing. It was a time when kids and youngsters were free of their parents. We saw our parents at mealtimes and in the evening, before being coerced into bed. Some of the parents bought the goods we stole in town: leather jackets, handbags, wrist watches, transistor radios, that sort of thing. Some of the children stole money from their parents; we were never short of money, never short of anything. Whatever we lacked, we got from the shops or from other places. The streets were ours, as well as the forests and mountains and the lakes in them, and the rivers, the whole of the magnificent countryside that surrounded the blocks and the detached houses by the sea. The children stayed outdoors, their parents indoors. One summer's day some teenagers were sitting on the flat rocks at Utnehagen grilling sausages, smoking and fishing in the sea, when Rune Carlsen came rowing up in a boat he'd borrowed, an old wooden boat with four oars: Did anyone want to come out for a row? We were sitting or lying in the sun when Rune shouted to us. I'd got myself a girl-friend at Laksevåg and was keen to row. I sat down behind Rune in the boat and grabbed the oars. Where are we going? he asked. We're going to Laksevåg, Rune. We rowed out from Utnehagen, near Biskop-shavn, crossed the current in the fjord and rowed with all our strength towards Nordnespynten. By about half way we were exhausted, rested on our oars. Rune wanted to turn back. But now turning back was as far as going on, we continued rowing. We rowed for all we were worth against wind and current and, after an exhausting hour, rounded Nordnes and rowed in towards Laksevåg. Totally depleted. We let the boat drift a while in Laksevåg harbour. Then Rune tied the boat up at the quay and we walked up Alleen near Damsgård, crossed Fyllingsveien and went up Nylundsveien to the house in Svingen where we picked up Eli for the bonfire party at Utnehagen that evening.

Many of the people I grew up with at Hellemyren still live there, or have moved back, home, from other places; we meet just as we used to, but we meet one another with children, and nowadays children are inseparable from their parents, we run around after our children as if they're our best friends. But they're not. We run around with our children who are our new friends. Today the streets and the forests and the mountains and the lakes are there, all that grandiose scenery that surrounds the residential blocks and the detached houses by the sea, occupied by parents playing with their new friends.

Øyjordsveien: the road has its genesis down in a hollow, not far from Hellemyren, three miles north of Bergen, and its termination high up, on the mountainside, like a river in reverse.

The road snakes up from the filling station down in the bottom (perhaps the road's original starting point was the sea but now it seems to be the petrol pumps) and makes its first right turn after the high-rise with the supermarket on the ground floor and five storeys of sheltered accommodation (my father lives here on the second floor); a building that enjoys a view of the football pitches at Stemmemyren. Here it's as if the road rests, or levels out before it takes another turn, to the left, a curve that climbs steeply providing a view of where the road has been; a four-lane motorway shoots in and out of the Eidsvåg Tunnel making exactly the same noise as the unceasing roar of a waterfall. You hear the waterfall but can't see it. After only the next bend, which describes a beautiful curve around the mountainside, the noise of the waterfall has gone and, here in this delta of stillness, the road divides—Skytterveien on the left, and on the right the road continues under its old name, in its original course, towards the farm of Ødejorden. Just how Ødejorden became Øyjorden, I can't say, but both names, Øde meaning deserted and Øy, an island, refer to the place; the old farm has lain abandoned, under the mountain of Hellefjellet, and it's not difficult to imagine that people really did live on an island, a strange island, because it's so high up, almost a mountain island, and it's like that today, the ground lies there isolated and protected, like some special secret place with its islanders and its mountain dwellers.

Like everywhere else, this area has been threatened by and exposed to development and expansion, and now several villas and linked houses occupy the space above which the old farm on its terrace still dominates the other dwellings. On this ledge, in an enlarged and renovated farmhouse, lives Atle Øyjord, I have no idea what he does, I never see him, even though he's my own age and a neighbour. I know nothing about him.

Below the old farm, on the right, was a school garden, which was listed, a lovely place where vegetables and flowers were grown in plots; it was a large, fenced-in garden, and then, two years ago all its trees and shrubs and flowers and vegetables were torn out by the roots and the ground was covered with gravel and partly asphalted and they built a gigantic box which we all thought was some sort of factory, but it was a nursery school.

Childhood is manufactured here.

The premises are enclosed with unclimbable wire fences and secured with a double-gate system which makes it impossible for the small prisoners to get out of the prison grounds.

We can see children tottering and crawling about the playground dressed in the sort of romper suits that cry out to have prison numbers printed on them.

We, the neighbours, the eyewitnesses, estimate that there could be between fifty and seventy children in this pre-school prison camp.

Øyjordsveien carries on past the nursery school, climbing steeply towards the last terraced houses and residential blocks at the road's end, an extremity marked by a metal barrier. Here the road ends, or perhaps not—a narrow gravel track leads from the terminus and takes the road like a side artery up into the mountains, the gravel road eventually turns into a path and the path climbs to the highest peak where startlingly, always overwhelmingly, even after you've travelled the path many times, you suddenly get a panoramic view of the whole of Bergen.

The boy stands on the highest boulder and looks down on the city hemmed in by the mountains. He's out of breath, panting, his heart thudding in his chest. He ran as fast as he could away from the house and up Øyjordsbakken, right to the top of the hill and on to the gravel road and up the path that's brought him here. He's pulled a jacket over his pyjamas, stands with his bare feet in slippers. It was only a few minutes ago that he got out of bed, a perfectly normal Sunday, he thought, his parents and sister sitting in the kitchen round the breakfast table when he came downstairs to eat with them. The cramped kitchen, the small kitchen table, he took his usual place on the bench against the wall, squashed in; he'd already got too large for this kitchen, for his bedroom, for the whole of the little house. And he was still growing. His body stretched, in both directions, his upper body and neck, his arms and legs, out of the short bed, out, towards the door, soon there'd be no room for him anywhere in the house. Everything inside him grew, everything on him grew, everything grew out of him. He was an appalled witness to the way his body changed, against his will, against his parents' will, they still treated him as if he were small, despite his becoming hirsute and ugly, a youth with hair on his face and everywhere else on his body. He tried his best to make himself smaller, fold himself, walk with a stoop. He tried his best to hide. But surely it was true that the quieter and more taciturn he became, and the longer and more frequently he avoided them and kept to his room, the more closely they monitored everything he did and said and kept him under surveillance, as if he were a criminal, as if he were concealing a crime, and they were just waiting for the moment when he gave himself away, when they could discover who he really was.

Who was he?

He didn't know himself.

But they knew, they knew only too well.

He'd just seated himself when his mother attacked: Why did you get home so late last night? Where were you? Your jacket smelt of cigarette smoke. He lowered his head, held his arms tight to his body. He shrank and swallowed the fury that was growing inside him. He didn't answer her, he said nothing. He began to eat a slice of bread. As you're out so much, and never tell us where you'll be or when you're coming or going, as you're almost never at home and obviously couldn't care less about anyone who lives here, why don't you just move out? his mother shouted at him. And at the words, MOVE OUT, he saw red. It was as if she'd dealt him a blow on a wound that was already hurting, a great gaping wound that was his face, that was his entire youth; all this enforced and inescapable imprisonment in a home, in a family, he jumped up and grasped the kitchen table with both hands and pushed the table towards her, over his mother.

He was fifteen.

He had no money, he was at school, how could he possibly move out, where would he go? This is my home.

The oilcloth slid off the table with plates and cups and glasses. Coffee and milk, bread and butter and newly-boiled eggs landed in his mother's and father's laps, he ducked behind his sister and ran past his father who'd stood up and tried to catch hold of him. He tore himself loose and ran up the stairs, locked the door of his bedroom, threw on a jacket and opened the window. Then he climbed out, he lowered himself, let go, fell. He fell to the ground. He hit the gravel and fell again, it was painful, it was good, he got to his feet and began to run. He ran in slippers and pyjamas covered with the jacket, up the steep hill, it was like running up a fast-flowing river, he was running against the current, sprinting with all his might to the mountain lake and the rock where he could rest. The boy looks down towards the city, it seems so small, so cramped. He lies down on the grass, in the soft moss, feels the dampness and a strong feeling of happiness that hurts—he's cold, he's wet and he's free.

If he can just get out of the house, out of the city, if he can just bear cold and pain, if he just faces the things that are difficult and tough, if he's strong enough to leave and be alone, then he'll be free. He can't go home until it's late, until night comes, perhaps he'll have to wait until morning and his parents leave for work, then he'll climb through his window like he's done so many times before, but this time he'll pack some of his clothes and things in a ruck-sack, and then he'll leave.

Øyjordsveien peters out on the mountain top with views of Bergen. The city lies there as it's done for centuries, with new houses and buildings and roads, it's not hard to imagine what it must have been like living there in the fourteenth, sixteenth and nine-teenth centuries. The city alters but the inhabitants, seen from a distance, from a mountaintop, are the same. They are the same characters with the same names and the same stories. From the mountain and the rock with its view of the city, I can also see the terraced house where my parents lived, Øyjordsveien 64; I live there now. The house is virtually unchanged, inside or out, I've kept everything as it used to be, the little kitchen with its kitchen table and its blue oilcloth, the living room and its furniture, the wall-paper and the curtains, the carpets and lamps, and a few months ago it was my daughter who moved out; she didn't want to live at home any more and went to Oslo.

My daughter's move was one of the hardest things I've had to bear. I don't know whether all parents feel the same way, maybe some are relieved that their child, the young adult, is on the move at last, has left the house, but for me it was a shock and I haven't got over it yet. Why a shock? Wasn't it expected? Yes, it was expected, it's natural that children leave home, it's necessary, but when it happens, it feels so brutal. Of course, I can't say this to her, and when she told me she wanted to leave, I immediately said that it was an important decision, that I quite understood, that I would have done the same myself and so on, I even trotted out one of my maxims: Everyone should live in the capital for a few years at some point in their lives. Did I mean it? Yes, I meant it, but now sitting here by myself, I could eat my own words. That first evening I sat alone in the living room, both my daughter and my girlfriend had moved out of the house, almost simultaneously, and gone to Oslo, I sat with my head in my hands feeling sorry for myself. I wept, repeating out loud (there was no one who could hear me after all): How could you both leave me like this? I, who've done my best for you all these years, I said, who've given you all my love and nearly all my time, and you just move out and leave me sitting here all alone like this.

How can you, at the age of almost fifty, adapt to an empty house?

How can you deal with your own loneliness, what can you fill it with?

How can you live?

I don't know, I don't know.

On Loneliness

I once confided to a friend (my only friend) that I was lonely. He immediately retorted: You don't even know the meaning of the word!

A lonely person doesn't think that others are familiar with loneliness; he is the only one who is lonely.

You don't become lonely by being alone. It's when you've got used to living with a lover and children and all the surrounding family and friends, it's when you suddenly lose all this, all these things you've become fond of and reliant on, that you become lonely.

You become lonely at a certain age. The children move out, your parents have grown old or are approaching death or they've already passed away. Your friends, too, have gone. You don't know why. Some of them are dead perhaps, some of them have simply disappeared; you've lost them or neglected them, or if you're lonely: You've driven them away.

At a certain age you can't be bothered with friends, and you can't bear being alone, either.

At a certain age you've had enough of everything, you've travelled too much, seen too much, you've visited too many cities. Most of what you do is repetitive, and repetition is painful: what you once experienced has vanished and you stand there like a stranger in a strange city that once you loved. You stop travelling. You'd rather be at home. The only way of overcoming the emptiness of repetition is to fill that repetition with further repetition—you do the same thing day after day.

So, by repeating yourself each day, you survive your lonely self. You survive by brushing your teeth, washing yourself, getting into and out of your pyjamas. A lonely person endures by switching lamps off and on, reading a book, making meals, taking a walk, the same walk every day. And then a cup of coffee. Then a cigarette. And this perpetual dialogue with yourself about which clothes to wear in the evening. Until you finally decide to put on the same ones as always—that's the simplest and easiest, always to dress in the same clothes.

The lonely person goes out.

There are days when he doesn't speak to a living soul. He talks to people who are dead, or to those who aren't there, every day he speaks to someone who isn't there.

Sometimes he speaks to cats and birds, to trees and bushes. He can stoop to talking to stones and clouds. He talks to his mother, he talks to his mother every day. Does he miss her? No, he's glad she isn't there, but he misses her all the same. He goes out of the front door, down the gravel path, stops at the mail boxes. No post. Good. He opens the gate, turns to the right, just like yesterday and every other day he turns to the right past the Linda Maria house. It's empty. Naturally, she's at work. Most sensible people are at work, that pleases him. This emptiness of the houses, the silence in the streets pleases him. He is alone, almost, with the streets and the houses. He walks down Øyjordsveien and up Skytterveien, past the low-rise and high-rise blocks where he grew up. He has so many memories of this street that he doesn't dwell on a single one. He walks quickly past the blocks and takes the path that leads down towards Sandviken Hospital, a psychiatric hospital, now being extended and growing in height and area, new wards and new storeys, new buildings in what has become a city within a city. One day—it was last month—he'd met an author who was walking with two men, and he asked who the two men were: They're my two minders, she said. They're making sure I don't abscond. She must have gone mad, he thought and gave her a hug before hurrying off towards the old town, Gamle Bergen, entering through the old city gate, across the cobblestones and past the house that Cecilie Løveid had moved into. Today, like all days, he walks past the house where Cecilie Løveid lives. It's a small house. White. It's strange that when you enter this house, in the evening, everything seems bigger and more open inside the house than outside it—the city, the narrow, dark, pent-up city, Bergen. He walks towards the city centre, following the waterfront and notices the tang of salt and damp woodwork. Here is the rope walk, a salt store, fish processing plants and the warehouses standing rotten and crooked at the water's edge. The things he sees while walking arouse no feelings in him, he walks, he has walked this route so many times that it's almost as if he's doing it blindly, with half-closed eyes, he tries his best almost not-to-see as he walks along. He's resting. What's he thinking about? He walks past the old slaughterhouse, Bergen Kjøtt, beneath the window of Åshild's studio, what's she drawing at the moment? He swings his arms. The sun is shining, there are boats in the harbour. The lonely man lights a cigarette, enters the iron gates of Bergenhus Fortress, crosses the newly mown lawns and walks in the shade of the trees that form an avenue leading to Håkonshallen and the Rosenkrantz Tower, out through the old City Gate towards Bradbenken and Bryggen. He lived here for several years, too, in Dreggsallmenningen, but he hardly ever thinks about that, as if that apartment and that time were part of another life and not his own. He wasn't the one who lived there, not the lonely man, it was someone else; and he overtakes himself as if he's overtaking any chance stranger.

He's approaching his destination.

He always follows the same streets through the city, buys a newspaper, folds it and walks down what he calls his favourite street, Olav Kyrresgate, it starts, as far as he's concerned, at the corner with the bookshop, and ends, abruptly, in the almost unfrequented cafe which he enters. In just a few hours now he'll be home.

On Travelling

One day, it must have been about twelve years ago, I phoned Klaus Høeck and asked him if he would read at a poetry festival in Bergen. He was amicable and reluctant: One doesn't get any younger, he said; I don't travel any more. At the time I didn't understand what I now understand only too well: You've done all your travelling, seen what you wanted to see, and what you haven't seen, you can't be bothered with. Last month I declined a trip to China. And it's only a few days since I turned down an invitation to go to India. I'd already said no to readings in the USA. And before that I put off travelling through Mexico with Morten Søndergaard and Thomas Boberg. From now on, I thought at the time, I'll make all my journeys in my own living room.

Just getting out of bed is like placing your feet on dry land after a long sea voyage. The ground sways, or is it your legs, they're shaking. You find yourself a long way from where you were yesterday.

Maybe you're not quite awake, but even the bathroom seems alien, as if you've woken up in a hotel in Sidi Ifni, it's dawn, you hear the calls to prayer from the local minaret. So it's too early to get up, and you return to bed. Now the journey continues unintentionally to a place you've never been before, and which you have no desire to visit, not yet, here, in this lovely, bright, sun-filled place, you meet your mother again, and she's been dead for twenty years. Like some restless Odysseus you struggle out of this dream and into another, only to wake bathed in sweat in a room just outside Dubrovnik. You turn to your girlfriend in the bed beside you, but she isn't there, where is she, is she already up, is she breakfasting alone in the town; it's two years since she left you. You wake up alone. Isn't this your own bed? If so, you're at home, where have you been, where are you heading today? You're heading out to the kitchen to have breakfast.

Of all spaces I like ships' cabins best, preferably in the bowels of the vessel, not far from the engine room; you can hear the engine beating like a heart.

There are no windows in the cabin. When you switch off the light, in the ceiling and above the bed, it's completely dark, totally black.

This ship leaves Helsinki and will arrive in Stockholm tomorrow. The cabin is plain, a bunk bed (should you lie above or below, it's best to lie below, under another bed, unoccupied on this short journey, lying beneath an empty bed feels comforting and secure, like sleeping under a staircase that no one uses), a small bedside table, a lamp and a bathroom with a basin and shower and toilet. That's all. That's all you need in a room; you turn off the light in the cabin, lie in the darkness and hear the engine throbbing, like a heart. Maybe you're journeying back to your mother, to inside your mother; I've never felt a greater sense of contentment than that rocking, thumping, dark crossing in the bottom of a ship.

Helsinki. What do you want there?

Nothing. There's nothing I want in Helsinki. I wanted and needed to get away from Bergen, that's all. I spent most of my time in Helsinki lying in bed in my hotel room. It's delightful lying in a hotel room in a city you've never visited before.

I was going to meet Szilvia Molnar in Stockholm. The ship arrived in the morning, it was Friday, 22 July, and my daughter rang three times from Oslo before I answered my mobile phone. She was crying. She was on the quayside at Aker Brygge, she said, together with loads of others who'd run out there, towards the sea. What's happened? I asked. She'd been at work in the clothes boutique, she explained, when the plate glass window blew in. It was an explosion, a powerful explosion, I thought there'd be more and that I was going to die, she said. The shop was filled with broken glass, broken glass everywhere, we were told to run, and outside in the street a crowd of people was running, a stream of running people and I ran out into the crowd and we ran towards the sea, she said. You're not hurt? I asked. No, she said.

I flew from Stockholm to Oslo. I took the train from the airport to the city centre. Oslo city was unrecognizable, silent, completely silent, and there was nobody in the streets, a terrible silence in the streets. The city was altered, I couldn't tell what by, but the place I found as I walked through its deserted streets one summer's evening in July was a totally different city to the one I knew.

Was that your last journey? Was it because of what happened in Oslo, that you ceased travelling?

I still travel, but not very far. I travel mainly back and forth between Bergen and Oslo, to visit my daughter. It's a beautiful journey, especially if you take the train.

You get on the train in Bergen, take a window seat on the right side of the carriage. You look out of the window. The train rolls out of the station, that first movement is nice, you're leaving the city. The journey is predictable, that's good. You're hauled out of the city, past Store Lungegårdsvann whose waters are grey and white-whipped by rain. The city recedes, it goes dark, the train runs into the mountain, the first tunnel, the start of an irregular rhythm of light and dark, in and out of tunnels. You look at your fellow passengers. You read a book. You rest. Rest at speed. The quicker the train goes, the more relaxed your body, and gradually your thoughts become calm. The train accelerates. It's a joy to read when going fast, it's as if the static sentences derive force and weight from the rapidity of the landscape flashing past; mountains and valleys, the fjord following the railway line, until, contrary to all geography and logic, it rises and turns into a river, you travel against the grain of the country and alter nature completely; the river climbs, the trees run and the mountains move rapidly in a manner which would be unthinkable if you weren't looking at them from the train window.

The conductor arrives, you show your ticket. At a fixed time, which isn't a place, you'll have a cup of coffee. You'll eat the sandwiches you've made specially for this journey; four slices of bread and cheese. At Finse station, the highest point on the journey, 1,222 metres above sea level, on the plateau, in the mountains, still with a covering of snow, an endless white sea of snow, and where the train halts for a few minutes, you alight from the train, and smoke a cigarette on the platform. You smoke. You get cold. Then the conductor blows his whistle, waves his flag and you climb back inside the carriage, the warm compartment.

On Sleeping

Now the train rolls or speeds downhill towards the east, from the west, towards Oslo. The boundary between east and west isn't obvious on the ground, but you see the frontier clearly in the sky; at a certain point, which is always the same, the clouds thin and the sky turns blue. The sun shines in through the train window. The traveller closes his eyes. If he's lucky, he'll fall asleep. If he's lucky, he'll sleep through the final, flat and very dull run into the capital. He'll be sleeping in Nesbyen and in Hønefoss. He'll be sleeping in Vikersund. Just before the traveller falls asleep, he thinks of the time he was at a concert in the Grieghallen with his girlfriend; they were listening to Gustav Mahler's Fifth Symphony, but somewhere during the long, flat and extremely slow Adagio, he fell asleep. Janne nudged him; how can you sleep now, she said, we're in the middle of the slow, beautiful quiet movement, as she called it.

But, he rejoined, that's just the perfect movement to sleep in. He often used to go to sleep at the theatre, and almost always at the cinema, and he thought how pleasant it was to sleep like that, surrounded by people, in an auditorium. It was nice sleeping next to a loved one, amongst strangers, in a soft seat, in the semi-darkness. He often dozed off on the bus, or on the train, or in the air, on a plane. In bed at night, on the other hand, at home, when everyone else was asleep, he could lie awake, it wasn't unusual. Just before he falls asleep, the train traveller thinks back to an Italian journey he made with another girlfriend; she'd phoned a car hire firm and asked if they needed any cars positioned, and they had one, a Peugeot 504, that had to be returned to Luxembourg. They were given three days to drive the car from Bergen to Luxembourg, and they'd continued by rail, he recalls, on Women's Day, the 8th of March. From Luxembourg they took the train to Italy, to Rome, and from Rome they proceeded by bus to Orvieto where they were to visit a couple of friends: he was an old and very eminent painter, she a young actor, they shared a summer cottage in Orvieto. The old artist was a real patriarch, the two girls would go out to prepare food in the kitchen, and the painter sat on the patio with the traveller discussing literature, philosophy, painting and politics. They talked and drank wine. All at once the discussion was over, the painter was tired, he wanted to sleep, a little nap before dinner, he said. Now we'll sleep, he said and shut his eyes, and in that instant he fell asleep. The traveller was amazed. He'd never seen anything like it; perhaps the old man was a kind of prophet for sleepers. He knew the mysteries of sleep and had a divine gift: when he said sleep, he slept. The traveller falls asleep. He sleeps until the conductor's voice over the Tannoy announces that the train will shortly be arriving at Oslo Central.

Not long after you get there, you're going back again. After only two days in Oslo the traveller is going home to Bergen. But this time he wants to take the night train. There's nothing nicer than spending the night in a sleeper, on a night train across the mountains: you go to bed in Oslo and wake up in the same bed in Bergen. The notion of falling asleep in one city and waking in another is always a little disquieting, always perplexing, until you've shaken off your drowsiness and recall that you're not in an ordinary bed, but in a bed that travels.

The night passenger buys a half bottle of wine and a baguette in the bistro car. He takes his bread and wine to the small compartment that fills him with such feelings of pleasure. It's practically a prison cell, a narrow bunk, a small basin, a window. This is where he's to sleep. Shut in, imprisoned, but in motion, sleeping, maybe he'll dream about keys, he often does. But before he goes to sleep, he wants to enjoy the cramped compartment. He opens the window. Smokes a cigarette in the small aperture that provides ventilation, the train swishes on through the darkness. He has a glass of wine, eats, and smokes another cigarette at the window; what is he thinking about? He's thinking about his daughter in Oslo, feeling how the distance between them increases with every turn of the train's wheels, he's being borne away homewards in the wrong direction.

On Keys

At one time, about fifteen years ago, I had a lot of keys, today I've only got one. Fifteen years ago, I kept all my keys on a key ring: the key to the flat in Dreggsallmenningen, the keys to the front door and the mail box there, the key to my parents' house in Øyjordsveien, the key to the house on Askøy, the key to the cabin in Sunnfjord and the key to the cabin on Sotra, the key to my girlfriend's flat in Michael Krohnsgate, and the key to a bank box. Now the houses and properties have been sold, the people who lived there are dead, or they've moved away, or I've lost contact with them, and the places they own are closed to me. Today I have only one key, and that's the key to the house I live in. I often dream about keys, also about the key ring I carried around with me for years, in my jacket pocket, or in my bag, constantly afraid that I'd lose the keys. I dream that I'm standing in front of a door and I get the heavy key ring out of my jacket pocket, but of all the many keys none fits the door I'm facing—I can't get in. This nightmare is repeated in many variants: I'm standing in front of various houses, assorted doors, with keys on strings or clips, sometimes I'm a teenager sometimes an adult, but the dreams have one thing in common, that they're all true—I really do possess all these keys and they don't open any doors.

I've made four copies of the only key I use now. I've given one key to my father and one to my daughter, a spare is hidden in a secret place near the door, and the last is on a cord attached to my trousers. One of my greatest fears, is to be unable to get into the place where I live. What would I do? The thought of being shut out takes me right back to my youth when I was sometimes thrown out of the house and had to spend the night outdoors, walking or sleeping under the stars. Walking about at night, sleeping under a tree might be regarded as freedom, but nowadays I'm too old to sleep in the forest or on a rocky ledge, and so it's always with a deep sense of gratitude that I feel my key slide easily into the lock, and turn, that the door opens, that no one shouts or screams, and that now I can walk quietly into the house where I live.

One day there was a letter from Szilvia in my mailbox. I waited three days before opening the letter. I waited until it was Friday, that's the day I open the letters that come: the week is almost over, it has passed without interruption, now I can open my letters, letter. I met Szilvia two months ago at a literary festival at the Louisiana Museum near Copenhagen, she was Sofi Oksanen's Swedish agent. At first I hadn't noticed her, even though she was constantly at Sofi's side, often hand in hand with Sofi who was strikingly made up and had added dyed hairpieces to her own hair which was wild, she'd strung small ornaments and pearls in her hair and around her neck, and she wore two skirts and two jackets over a white, frayed blouse and black, holed tights—a costume so eye-catching that it almost completely hid her. I talked to Sofi as often as I could, we'd both been nominated for the same literary prize, and I'd just read *Stalin's Cows*. We spoke in English, and it was only when I said something out of place and Sofi flared up that her Swedish agent stepped in to calm the situation. That was Szilvia. Now I saw her. Szilvia Molnar. She introduced herself, took me by the arm, led me aside, offered me a cigarette. Sofi doesn't swim, she said, but I'd like to go swimming with you, is it far to the beach, how do we get there? We've got to bike there, I said, it's about three miles, I cycle and swim every morning, before breakfast, it's early, I said giving her the opportunity to back out. She nodded. I can't ride a bike, she said, but I'll try.

I barely slept a wink that night. I lay there thinking
of Szilvia who couldn't ride a bike and who'd have
to undress and dress on the beach. Were we really
going to swim together, I was certain she wouldn't
turn up at the appointed hour, and when she wasn't
at reception at eight o'clock or a quarter past, I felt
relief; it's good that she's not coming, that I won't be
confused, disturbed, that I don't feel anything for
anyone, I thought as I went out of the hotel door to
fetch my bike. Szilvia was sitting there on a bench,
she slept, was half asleep? She opened her eyes and
gazed at me with such weariness and familiarity that
it made me think we'd spent the night together, that
we'd been together a long time, that we were lovers,
a couple. I've been waiting for you, she said.

Tomas, she said, I can't cycle or swim, it's the honest
truth, she said, and then we started off towards the
beach. Tomas, she shouted, behind me, I'm riding a
bike! I didn't turn round. We rode towards the sea.
Left the bikes on the beach. Walked along the sand
and found some cover behind a sand dune, undressed,
got into our swimming things. I didn't look at her. I
tried my hardest not to look at her. We ran to the sea,
threw ourselves into the breakers. Tomas, she yelled,
I'm swimming!

It was impossible not to fall in love.

As we rode back towards the hotel, to breakfast, she shouted again. Tomas, I lied to you back there on the beach. The way she kept repeating my name, and now was saying that she'd lied to me, it seemed so intimate, so well-remembered, so normal and confiding; I could no longer maintain any distance from this woman who was pedalling after me with her long legs, long body and long hair whipping around her beautiful face; I was in love. Tomas, I lied to you back there on the beach when I said I didn't write, I do write, she said.

That day we went to a Sophie Calle exhibition together, at the Louisiana Museum: Take Care of Yourself. Sophie Calle had received a letter in which her lover said their affair was over, he ended the letter by saying: Take care of yourself. Sophie Calle made copies of the letter and passed them on to girl-friends and well-known women who interpreted the letter and commented on it while Calle filmed them, it was all these films and photographs of women reading that made up the exhibition; was it some sort of revenge, or was she working through an unhappy love affair, was art Sophie Calle's way of taking care of herself?

Szilvia and I sat in the Louisiana cafe exchanging addresses, we didn't know each other, and yet it was as if this one day was linked to other days, days before and after the one on which we'd met. She rolled up her left sleeve, showed me a tattoo on her forearm. She'd had the outline of a key tattooed on the skin above her main artery. I'm flying home tomorrow, Szilvia said; I'll write you a letter, and in it I'll let you in on a secret, she said.

The letter arrived a couple of months later, on a Tuesday, I opened it on Friday, in the morning, read the letter and reread it. Then I rose quickly from the kitchen table, let myself out and retrieved the spare house key, it was hidden under a stone near the steps to the porch door. I put the key in an envelope, wrote a short note and placed it in the envelope with the key. Then I ran out of the house, down the gravel path and through the gate, turned right down the twisting road to the shop where there's a letterbox. I bought stamps, stuck them on the envelope and posted the key to Szilvia's address in Stockholm.

On the Necessity of a Door

You shut the door. After some hours, two, three hours, you open the door and emerge, altered? Not much, but you are slightly changed, and even though it's almost invisible, almost imperceptible, these hours behind a closed door can have big consequences.

.

When the Espedal family moved out of their high-rise flat in Skytterveien and into the linked house in Øyjordsveien, I got my own room. A room of my own with its own door, my door, the door to my room. It was a big change, but not big enough to satisfy my aims and desires, it was the start, of what? I didn't know, but it was the start, perhaps of my youth, of my need to rebel, my yearning for freedom, even though freedom was limited at that moment to being shut in a room. Shutting yourself in, isn't that the start of freedom? But in this first room of mine there was still a remnant of childhood, of oppression, because I couldn't lock the door. The door of my room flew open whether I wanted it to or not; my sister, my father, or worst of all, my mother, could come barging into my room at any time. The solution to this was simple, but long in coming, it would be months before I discovered it was possible to purchase a hook and eye, the hook screwed into the door frame and the eye into the door itself. From now on nobody could enter my room unannounced. They had to knock, shout or kick the door, and even that wasn't enough, I didn't open up. They used threats. If you don't open this door now, immediately, at once, you can just stay in there, you'll be grounded, or: if you don't open this door straight away, you'll get no meals and no pocket money. Even this had no effect. Your father will break the door down, my mother yelled. But he didn't, wouldn't. My father respected a lock, in the same way he respected laws and traffic regulations. My room had a window. This window became my door, a first floor door, ten feet above the ground, but a door nonetheless; I got or climbed in and out of the window. Now, at the age of fifteen, I was almost a free and independent person, locked in, but with two doors of my own.

Seventeen years later I was married, and the woman I married got a job in Nicaragua and we were given a house in Matagalpa and that house had no doors. Or rather, the house possessed a splendid front door, but inside the house, between the rooms, there were no doors.

An architectural ideal: rooms flowing into one another, a short flight of steps up to the kitchen which was open to the living room, a hole in the wall leading to the bedroom, another hole to the guest room and a longer staircase to a workroom on the first floor. This room could be mine, it could be lovely: a big, bright room with a slanting ceiling and large windows; I could furnish it with a desk, a bunk, lamps, books, everything I needed to be at peace, secluded, but the room lacked a door.

The architect must have designed the house for an open family, a couple who loved one another, who co-operated and respected one another and who had a happy and transparent relationship, but this wasn't the case in my new family; I needed a door.

We furnished the house according to clear and set principles: this is a living room, here is the dining room, and the corner over there is a work station, through there is the bedroom, and behind the curtain, which we put up, was the guest room. I secretly (why secretly?) ordered a door from the local joiner. I asked for a door with a lock, and the door was brought to the house and installed with its frame in the opening to my workroom on the first floor. The woman I'd married was at work when the door was delivered and hung, and when she got home, an hour before we were to fetch our daughter from the childminder, Elise Morales, I was sitting locked in my room working, I was writing. I heard my wife enter the house, she walked around downstairs for a while, then came up to the first floor, and I heard her halt and give a sigh. A deep sigh. Had she foreseen and expected this door? She took a step forward, put her hand on the door handle, turned it suddenly and tugged as hard as she could at the door.

In the course of a few seconds I was whisked far away from where I sat in my room in Matagalpa; a journey of lightning speed through time and space, across many years, seventeen years back in time and thousands of miles away; I was, in the time it took for a few kicks to land on the locked door, back in my boyhood bedroom in Øyjordsveien.

In some respects a life undergoes no development: we get older, we've gained experience and some understanding, we've travelled and met people, read books and risen to challenges, we've got wiser, but at the same time we remain that same obstinate child, that small person who finds such pleasure and a certain freedom in locking himself in a room.

I was a boy, aged thirty-two. I ought to have been, should have been, a man, responsible, married, a father, author, but I sat there then feeling so content, happy almost, at having locked myself in my room.

There was a larger and stouter and much more impenetrable door between the two of us, my wife and I, than that thin wooden door in Nicaragua. After a few months we divorced, it was a relief to both of us, we could each travel back to our own loneliness, or to new relationships, to new doors, new rooms.

The Writer's Evening

I'd really like to live in Spain. Wake up with the sun on my face. Have breakfast outdoors in the warmth on a small stone patio. Shadows from an acacia tree. Poppies fluttering in the breeze like frocks. A view of the sea. The hard blue that hurts the eyes. The snow-decked mountains behind the house. It's nice to think of your native land when you're not living there.

I'd really like to have a car. Preferably a slow, solid British car with leather seats and a dashboard in walnut. Glove compartments full of tablets and amphetamines. Ashtrays in the doors. And those tinted windows you can see out of, but not into. A hook to hang my jacket on. A courtesy light and a small writing table.

I'd really like to start a revolution.

I'd really like to be able to raise two or three people from the dead.

I'd really like to own a revolver.

If I could meet just one dead person, it would be my mother.

I'd go around in a black suit with a black velvet shirt and black boots. A wide-brimmed hat. A stick fashioned from cedar with a silver handle. If I saw O.H.H. appear over the brow of the hill, I'd shoot him dead on the spot.

It feels good to have enemies. It keeps you young and uncooperative.

I don't miss having a girlfriend, I miss Janne.

I'd really like to have known Sylvia Plath.

I should have gone to Berlin in November 1989. Visited friends in Charlottenburg and cycled with them to the Brandenburg Gate to watch the people smashing holes in the Wall. Experience the song of history. The winds of change. A historian friend often remarks that the Wall coming down was probably the last chance we had to experience the song of history; I think he's wrong: It won't be long before there's a revolution in Europe.

I come from a good family. That sentence is a short story in itself.

If I'd been able to choose which side of the Berlin Wall to live on, I'd have lived in the east, preferably in Karl Marx Allé, in one of the blocks of flats there. I'd have worn a uniform. And I'd have been an informer, I'm certain of that.

I'd really like to be forced to live in the same place all my life. With a wife and children, a small family.

We wouldn't need much, the basic foodstuffs, cloth-
ing, some work. My wife might be a teacher. I'd
work for the Party, as a journalist. In the evening I'd
keep diaries. Always, wherever you are, you have to
live a secret life.

In the summer of 2010, Narve and I went to Albania.
We took a small Albanian ferry from Corfu, and
about half way across we could look back on the
Venetian palaces of Corfu and ahead towards the
apartment blocks and high-rise buildings of the Albanian coast. The wind got up and the sea turned
rough, on the boat's deck a lone car, a Mercedes, had
been lashed fast and began, despite its moorings, to
slip sideways, the boat listed, and all of us passengers
were afraid the boat might capsize and sink. Narve
and I stood on deck, ready to hurl ourselves into the
sea, and start swimming: Which way would you go?
I asked. Towards Greece, he replied. I'd make for
Albania, I said.

In Albania we travelled to Gjirokastër and looked
for Ismail Kadare's house. We found the house but
had no key. After hours of searching and effort we
found the woman who had the key to the house. She
unlocked the door. The house was empty. Full of dust
and rubble. We looked at each other in disappointment. What did you expect? the woman asked.
She was a teacher. Kadare lives in Paris, she said. In

Paris he writes books about Albania, always Albania in his books. If you want to see Kadare's house in Gjirokastër, you'll have to read his books, she remarked dryly.

As we stood in the open doorway, two men came walking up. They were looking for the house of Ismail Kadare. This is the house, I said, and it's empty. The two men looked at each other in disappointment. What did you expect, the teacher woman said in English, it was obvious she'd rehearsed this lecture about Kadare and Gjirokastër; she clearly revelled in all the travellers who came from afar looking for something that wasn't there. Past is past, she said didactically. Today no one here cares about Kadare's house. Ten years ago there were still people vandalizing the house, or trying to set fire to it, but now there's nothing to trash or set fire to, the house is made of concrete, and over there, she said pointing to a square hole in the concrete wall, was a window and in front of it was Kadare's writing table.

Was she smiling? Yes, she smiled as she pointed to the absent writing table. The writing table had surely been smashed to splinters, and set on fire, a little bonfire on the floor of the workroom, the same with his books, the same with his furniture and beds, a great bonfire in the Kadare house.

The two men introduced themselves, they were Ole and Enckel. Ole was a journalist from Germany, he lived in Berlin, had a Swedish mother and completely blonde hair, shoulder-length almost white hair above a sunburnt face, blue eyes and a reddish beard; he resembled a seaman, or an adventurer, perhaps he was both. Enckel, unemployed, came from Tirana but was now working as Ole's driver, he was short had a crew cut, a wide face, large mouth, broad shoulders, muscular arms. He didn't look like a driver, more a bodyguard, perhaps he was neither. Most people here, as we had already learnt, weren't just one thing, but many; the man who'd pointed us towards the teacher with the house key, was a historian and car mechanic, he ran a kind of guest house and could change money, he also sold carpets. Ole and Enckel drove round Albania searching for stories that Ole could write up for German magazines. They'd parked down in the town, were driving to Tirana, did we want a lift in exchange for the petrol money, yes we did. The car was a silver-grey Mercedes that Enckel had borrowed or rented from his uncle. It soon became apparent that Enckel was a fast driver. This forced a confession from me, as the car shot up a narrow, one-way street, increasing speed, I leant forward in the back seat and shouted to Enckel: Please Enckel, I'm a writer with a daughter and two books I've got to write before I die. Enckel slackened speed. Ole lit a cigarette. Are you famous? he enquired. Not in Albania, I said. What do you write about? he asked. Monotony, I replied. Enckel thought this funny and speeded up. Monotony, he shouted, laughing and accelerating, it's hardly surprising you're not famous in Albania.

I'd really like to write a book about Tirana. About the women and the jazz clubs there. About the way we had to turn the clock back in Tirana, not an hour, but several decades, to the beginning of the sixties, just before the student riots, like the one in Paris. The suppressed, rebellious atmosphere of the streets, in the clubs, the music, the talk, the cigarettes, the black clothes in Tirana's basement dives, the beautiful men, and women; unbridled, scantily dressed, oppressed and free in the basements of Tirana. Coltrane and Miles Davis and Gypsy music in the basements of Tirana. Candles and semi-darkness and darkness and near blackness in the basements of Tirana. A clandestine life in those basements. But then we might find that we hadn't turned the clock back far enough, that things weren't right, decades weren't enough, we had to turn the clock back centuries; we weren't in Paris after all, weren't in the sixties, we were in Albania. One night we were sitting in the club listening to jazz and discussing politics when a youth was shot on a cafe terrace close by. Next day, while we were eating breakfast, Enckel explained that the boy had been given his death sentence as a fifteen-year-old, but that they had to wait until he was eighteen to carry out the sentence, and then they'd waited a few more years before shooting him, so that he could really find out what living with the fear of it was like, so he could really live with death before they killed him.

I'd like to be confined. We feel guilty. We deserve punishment. Most people would benefit from a spell behind bars.

In the spring of 2011, I ran a writing course at Bergen Prison. I drove out to the prison at Breistein, parked the car and walked towards the wall and the huge entrance gate where you're sluiced through a system of doors. You go past the first door as a free man, but after a couple more doors, you begin to understand what it might be like to lose yourself.

In one of the offices I was equipped with a personal alarm. I was advised not to ask the inmates why they were in prison. There were seven on the course. One woman. The man sitting at the desk nearest me, was bald, had an earring in each ear, tattoos, muscular arms, a powerful torso, almost abnormally so, as if it had been grown under glass, in a greenhouse. He had a speech impediment and said immediately, during the introductions, that he'd killed his girl-friend. There was already some chalk writing on the board, and when I asked the class if there was a sponge, the murderer got up from his desk, left the classroom and returned with a damp sponge and wiped away the words on the board, unfortunately just then I began to cry.

It wasn't necessary to ask the inmates what they were in for. They told me themselves, at the first opportunity. When, during the break, I stood in the prison yard smoking with Frank, he was missing some teeth and had a scar running from his ear diagonally down to his mouth, as if someone had attempted to sever his face in two, he told me that he came from a proud family, two people had injured and dishonoured his family; one of them had been killed, he'd get the other when he was let out.

After a few weeks I'd become fond of all the students on my course. I sometimes thought: It's a good thing I've got no position in society and that I control absolutely nothing and haven't got the keys to the doors and gates here, because if I had I'd set all my students free.

The one we called Wily had been sentenced for paedophilia. He chain-smoked in the breaks and rolled his cigarettes in the classroom, waiting only for the chance to light them: If it wasn't for the baccy, he said, I'd have been dead long ago.

Wily had been to sea. He'd sailed up the River Congo, where one of the ship's boys had vanished after shore leave in one of the villages: We never found him, he was eaten by local cannibals, Wily said. I said to my old woman you're starting to turn your back on me now, and you mustn't do that, or else I'll do something bad. But the wife didn't want me any more, and she goes on turning her back, every night, and then I done my first attack and it wasn't only my fault, it was her that made me do something wrong. Now I look after the flowers in here, see, out in the corner of the exercise yard there's a kind of garden with vegetables and stuff, and I'm the gardener, in a manner of speaking, for the prison flowers. I'd like to have written books, because I've got such a lot to tell, you know if I'd managed to put down everything I've been through, it would have made a hell of a good book, a real bestseller. I wouldn't have to teach idiots like us in prison the way you do. I've tried reading one of your books and the only thing I could see is that you're just as fond of little girls as me. There's no difference between us in here and you on the outside, we're just unlucky that's all, we've been unlucky all our lives, just real unlucky dogs.

Lisa would sit in the middle of the classroom, her hair always covered with a scarf, she said nothing, wrote nothing, every week she'd sit at her desk sketching portraits of us all, it was unsettling, as if we were sitting in a courtroom. As if we, the subjects of her drawing, were guilty of a crime.

Harald was good at writing. He looked like a perfectly normal youth and it was impossible to discover what he'd done; he never said anything about himself, and never wrote, like the others did, about things to do with his own life or crimes. He wrote short stories. Good short stories. They were of exceptional quality, and I looked forward to going through them and giving him positive feedback. But, after only three weeks he went absent from the class. I couldn't hide my disappointment: What's happened to Harald? I enquired. Why doesn't he come, why's Harald staying away? He's been let out, Frank said. Oh, that's a pity, I said, without thinking.

Frank began to laugh. Oh, that is a pity, he repeated. He sat tipping back in his chair as usual, his body at a demonstrative angle, his arms folded; he was the boss in the classroom, in the entire prison and beyond its walls, he was the one who dictated his own movements. I've always said we're well off in here. We get good food and care. I don't know why people moan all the time, whine and moan, and old Jonny boy here tries to kill himself the first opportunity he gets, well he did for his girl too; but there's no need to punish Jonny boy, because he punishes himself more than anyone. He might as well be out, because he carries his punishment inside himself and can never be free anywhere. Jonny boy isn't a danger to anyone except himself. He was a danger to his girl, but she's dead, and once you've killed the one you love most, you're no danger to anyone else. Jonny boy tries all he can to kill himself, but he's not allowed to, no, he's got to stay here and rot from the inside, said Frank rising from the chair he'd been tipping backwards. He walked to the desk where Jon sat silent and inert. I'd like to have killed you, Frank said, and for a moment I thought that the two giants were about to fall on one another, the two most dangerous men I'd ever seen, I expected them to hurl themselves into some mighty battle, did I hope so? I reached for my personal alarm, but Jon remained seated, it was as if he was gathering all his vast strength in an effort to sit still. But I've got someone else more important to deal with, Frank said and left the classroom.

Each time Frank walked out of the classroom, he was stopped by two prison officers who pushed him up against the wall and frisked him. He stood with his legs apart and his arms above his head and laughed as the officers went over his jacket and trousers and boots for weapons. If Jon really wanted to die, I thought, all he needed to do was attack Frank. But maybe, in their own way, the two men had become fond of one another, just as in my own way I'd become fond of them, as you do with others in prison.

On the last day in the prison, when the writing course was over and I'd thanked them for having me, Frank came up and wanted to smoke a cigarette in the exercise yard, we went out together, there was something he needed to tell me. I'm getting out quite soon, he said. Then I'll have to do what I've got to, but this time I'm going to do a runner, get out of the country, far away, somewhere in Africa, I can't do another stint in here, he said. I tried to look him in the eyes, but had to lower my gaze. Don't do it, please Frank, I said. Frank let out that hard, false laughter of his. Don't do it, please, he said mimicking my voice. You don't understand people like me and my family, we are warriors; always, everywhere, there's people who become warriors, and when there isn't a war, we make one, that's how it is and that's how it's got to be. As long as there are warriors, there must be wars, get it, no you don't, you don't get it at all because you've never been free and you've never been inside. Because you've never had to fight and struggle for anything at all. Everyone, and I mean everyone, would benefit from a spell inside, and specially people like you. I wish you were my brother, but you're not, he said slapping me hard on the back. That was the farewell. When the gates locked behind me and I got into my car to drive home, my arms and legs were paralysed, I couldn't start the car and just sat behind the wheel, in the car park outside the walls, until it began to grow dark.

Love

She came cycling
past
How could he know
the first time he saw her
that this movement
past
was her movement?

She cycled sitting upright
cycled so fast
that he couldn't possibly know
that he was to love her
more than anyone else
and that it wouldn't die
that it would never die
that he would love her
the rest of his life.

If he'd known this
maybe he'd have
let her cycle
past
without stopping her
but he stopped her
and he shouldn't have done that.
Or should he?

Could anyone in all the world say
that he wouldn't want to meet you
that he wouldn't want to fall in love with you
that he wouldn't want to be with you
that he wouldn't want to see you again
after watching you sleep
after seeing you wake
after seeing you
as you are
you are the loveliest person
he will ever meet
How could he say
that he didn't want to love you
that he didn't want to be destroyed by you.

Should he have said no
to love
because it could destroy him
Should he have said no
to you
because he could have continued
his life as himself
without destruction
without changes
without life;
you gave him love
only to take it away again.

They say that heartbreak passes
that time heals all wounds

but what if it's not true?
What if love endures
long after the affair is over
and love won't stop
even though it's over
between us
How will he live without her
with the sorrow
that won't get better
How will he live with the loneliness
that comes after he's been abandoned
by the one he wanted to share his life with
his whole life
the rest of his life
that was what he wanted
that was what he believed
that they'd be together for ever.

After more than two years alone
it suddenly struck him
it struck him like a thunderbolt
in the night one night
at Ronda
where he'd gone to get a real taste
of loneliness
that he was meant to be alone
in order to be together with her
for the rest of his life.
It was possible
in the hardest way

in the cruellest way
to be together with her
if he was alone.

Alone
for the rest of his life
yes
without her
for the rest of his life
with her
it was possible.

If he couldn't be together with her
then he wouldn't be together with anyone
else; he didn't succeed though.
His hands didn't want to
his mouth didn't want to
so why should he force his hands
and his mouth
to do something he didn't want?

At the age of fifty-one he made up his mind
to be together with her for the rest of his life
It was his great chance
to feel something enduringly bad
and enduringly good
a liberation
that could bind him fast to solemn life
that could force him down into the depths of life
into the deepest parts

into the hardest parts
it was necessary for him
he could finally become a lover.

Not to be loved
and to love
turned him into a lover.
He stood on the bridge
over the rushing river
at Ronda.
The waterfall
leapt through him
and flowed into stiller waters
it was quiet in the mountain village
cold and starry
the wind touched the trees
and they stilled.
He lit a cigarette
and felt for the first time
a deep accord
and love
for the world.

Ronda, April 2013

nain standing

ees   always already
                               entwined in each other
will remain standing   alone
istance   in bloom
shed   twice in fruit
ll remain standing   after I've
     the second time

                    ze

find it   and leave it

The place   take note of it
the pines and shadows beneath here the white
anemones rest
they close up in the rain in the dark in the cold   and
open
every day   every day
the stream flows past repeating the transition

The place opens   in trees
and flowers   and water   every single day
Take note of it   because one day you'll be
gone from the place where you live

That you are gone
is a gift
to those who remain

What bliss it is
to be nameless
without abode

You who could live only in one place
Now live everywhere

You who could love only those nearest to you
now at last love those who are furthest from you
here in your native spot you have no volition

You live   where you're supposed to
How nice it is to be put in   a place
without being able to decide things

What bliss it is to inhabit
the last place   which resembles that first one
where all was a beginning

Love loves to go   further

And you who remain
shall go further now than ever until you find the
place you knew even as a child   then the place
was there in your dreams a totally tangible place
like a clearing in the forest with a stream flowing
past   you'd
never been there but recognized the place you're
going to

And this place can be found in so many places. I passed it today here in the mountains behind Ronda: You follow an old stone paved road, over a bridge, out of the town, the road turns to gravel, almost red, before it changes colour and becomes a white path between the pines. And there, suddenly, heralded by flowers, by white anemones, the stream comes surging shiny over its bed of rock. It's your place, but not yet.

You follow the river a while and carry on up, up to the heights with their view of what you've left behind.

You've seen this view before
several times
when you were so keen to leave
But not any more
you want so much to remain
in several places

There's a cat in Ronda. The Torres family moved to Málaga and took their cat with them, but the cat didn't like Málaga, so they told me in Ronda, and one day it left the city and headed for the mountains. How many days did the cat travel, on the edge of the motorway or along unknown paths through the forest, across rivers, with no track perhaps, nothing but the route the cat followed under the trees and across great, open expanses? Past dogs. Wildernesses and plains and through flowery meadows, red fields of poppies and on up across the hills, over the tops, over the mountains, on its road now, to Ronda. Where did you sleep? What did you eat? What did you think about? The cat found the street and the house where it had lived and where a new family was living now. Every day the cat lay down on the front doorstep, and every day it was shooed away. During the day the cat makes its regular round of the village streets where many of the inhabitants know the cat's story and regard it as a hero, they put out leftovers of fish and other things and call the cat's name as it passes by. There's Romeo, they call, and tell visitors about the cat's great love for its home town.

And the woman in the neighbouring house, working on the patio, at a long trestle laden with fruit: oranges in boxes, lemons, apples, raspberries in baskets, strawberries, two basins of water, a knife. The washed clothes are already hanging on the line, and in the shade of the clothes, on the patio, the woman works at washing and peeling the fruit. She works on and on, it grows dark and she switches on a light above her. She cannot see it, but at her back a full moon looms between the mountains behind the house, a curious cleft in the landscape where two wooded hills plunge into a valley at the far end of which there rises, first a small white mountain, and behind it, a loftier black one pointing a white, snow-covered pinnacle at the yellow moon which illuminates the clouds beneath her.

It's warm here but the moon's light is cold
The sun, too, has its coldness
Today I've crossed two mountain passes
in mist and rain no visibility
sweated and shivered and rejoiced at how hard
it was to get here

How difficult it is to be here

But then I was given this room
with a small balcony
right above the woman on the patio
where the tables were spread with plastic tablecloths
and the boxes of fruit oranges lemons apples
it's my Cézanne vista.

I have nothing to bequeath
apart from this absence
which makes me belong to you

And this small walk in the village today
past gardens of clematis
growing so profusely so against all colours
To walk beneath the conifers
on a path of pine needles through the wood the groves
of olive trees lemon grass poppies red
orange orange trees in the gardens overgrown with
    weeds
wild flowers violet blue along the river that empties
in this bay of cliffs salt sea salt green

blue silver in the breakers white and black
Stone houses the mountains ranging round
in a hard form of protection
So much life
in the houses the gardens here
under the shadow of old age

You can't anticipate growing old here
age was not formed in you as a child
and now it's too late
to grow old

Yesterday I visited a poet's house
he lived here with his second wife
and their three children
You can't possibly live in a house
where a poet has lived
and so the house stands empty
fully furnished two desks dining room bedrooms
the bed was freshly made
The house was almost inhabited
but there's no one here
in the kitchen in the children's rooms in the work rooms
in the living room or in the garden where the apple
      trees blossomed

Death wasn't all that old in this house

How hard it is to live
together and alone

By the seashore
it's not a long walk
you follow a path so well trodden
so badly worn so scarred and white
that you can see the veins of water
beneath the thinning gravel so old
that you feel new as you walk
on the path beneath the pines
You pass an olive grove cross
a stone bridge and just as the path twists
you see the ocean you see the sea
beating in powerful pulses
against the rocks and cliffs in the bay
where the gulls scream and fight the wind
by the seashore
I stand and watch a pair of seabirds
resting
on the rough waves

Would not would would not would not would would
would not not would not would would not rest

You would not rest would move on
on
you would
I love you
and I always will
even after I'm gone.

Him

She wakes early, in her own bed, in her own room, in her own flat. She might say: my rooms. So good, so liberated, so bright, but hard, hard to move out, hard to leave, hard to break free, break in pieces, hard to destroy.

All this newness, all these possibilities, hard, but good. Necessary. My life, my rooms, my city, my trees. She might say: my outlook.

She sits in the kitchen, breakfast, alone, so new. A new life. She might say: my future. So open, so sunny, in the kitchen and on the patio, on the sofa and chairs, in the bed in the bedroom, my sun, my flat, my future. My spring. Two new dresses, new shoes. A new jacket. New cups, new glasses. A completely new pain. She might say: my choice.

Destroy, she says.

She drinks a cup of tea. She eats an apple. She cuts the apple into pieces with a knife. The sun shines through the kitchen window. It's Sunday. Sunday's the hardest day. To be tough. To be certain. To be alone. Don't phone, don't doubt, don't repent, don't cry, don't say anything to anyone. Stretch out the distance between them like an elastic band and hold the band taught, until the distance becomes permanent. Until the distance is so hard and tight that she can't see him clearly any more: He becomes indistinct, he becomes smaller, weak, no, not too weak, or she'll feel sorry for him. She feels sorry for him. She might say: My future, my life, my body, can't belong to one man.

She showers. She spends a long time in the shower. Beneath hot water. She misses the warmth. Not always him, but the warmth. The warmth of a body. Which body? She sleeps with a hot-water bottle in her bed. She showers for a long time, increasing the heat gradually. She'll manage alone for a while. How long? How long with this coolness, this distance, this loneliness. She might say: My distance, my coldness, my loneliness, they're necessary.

It's necessary to be alone. To break up. To begin again, a new place, my place, my life, in my hands. Not in his hand or in someone else's hands, not in anybody's hands or hand, my life is almost handless now, not even a finger in my life now, not so much as a fingernail that's not my own in my life now, my life is in my hands, she might say.

It's necessary. She looks at her hands.

Destroy, she says.

The sun is shining, it's raining, she sits at the kitchen table. She reads the letter, unfolds it, for the third time, reads and tears it up. She tears it to pieces, large at first, then smaller, then tiny pieces until the letter is disjointed words and letters. She could hurl them out into the room like snow. All these beautiful words. She can't use them for anything, not now. She doesn't need them, not now. She needs something else, something other than words, something totally different, she needs change.

She writes three words on a sheet of paper. She folds the paper and pushes it into an envelope. She puts his name on the envelope, in a new way, she disguises the writing a little, as if to make his name alien, or push it away from her and return it to him. It's his name, no longer hers. She has loved that name, but she doesn't need it any more and wants to send it away from her.

She's free. She can do what she wants. She doesn't always know what she wants; so much of the old life clings to her and makes her do the same things as she did before, old gestures and habits that went with being a couple, now she's single, is she sitting here waiting? for what? for whom? And why does she still move through the rooms as if there's another person in the flat? She must create some completely new movements for herself, her very own single-person movements. She must surprise herself. She sits on the sofa flicking through a travel brochure. She comes across a favourable mention of a hotel in Berlin. She's never been to Berlin. The hotel is old-fashioned and elegant, quiet and central, the review says, she doesn't know why, but she likes the hotel's name: Askanischer Hof, it reminds her of something, and she decides to go to Berlin.

Her

He wakes early. He's got an ashtray on his bedside table. He's got a lamp on his bed. He writes a lot of letters. He sends the letters to the same address.

He opens the bedroom window. He likes the house he lives in. He likes the garden. He likes the trees. He doesn't like living here alone.

It's been two years since she left him, and sometimes he still hopes that she'll come walking through the door like she used to. He's waiting for his broken heart to mend, but it doesn't. When she moved out of the house, he fell into a kind of stupor; love is one of the most beautiful things, but it can also destroy a person.

He's got to be careful about going anywhere. He may not be able to return home.

He can sit for entire days staring out of the window. Blue, lilac, pink, red, violet, yellow; the colours change, it's impossible to state that the colour red is the same in the morning as in the afternoon, and by the evening the reds have almost disappeared, they have sunk into a deeper hue, almost mauve, soon black. The colours go out. He switches on the lamp in the living room, and now the colours are back again, but they're indoor colours, and the red he observed in the flower outside, is paler inside, almost unrecognisable, as if the flowers and colours indoors have been robbed of the strength they had outside. He spends too much time in the house, and when he switches off the living room lights in the evening, he gets an inkling of how everything will turn colourless one day.

For a long time he's hoped for some harmless disease. A trivial illness, severe enough to keep him in bed for several weeks. He needs rest. He has the desire to feel sorry for himself. But after only a couple of days his temperature goes back down and he's well enough to get up, resume his work, take up his old habits once again. But all this makes him tired and he stays in bed to nurse the illness that laid him low for a few blissful days.

Magpies are building a nest in the garden. There are ants in the bathroom wash basin. Rats in the basement. The spider has spun her web, it's the season for flies and mosquitoes. The bees come in swarms. Their buzzing sounds like electricity, like the bulb in a street lamp just before it expires and goes out, and there's darkness. The swarm vanishes as quickly as it came. The wagtail has arrived, and the blackbird, the sparrow and the great tit. Of all the birds, he likes the wood-pigeons best, the powerful noise they make as they fly up. Yesterday he saw a hawk stoop from the sky, it came down on one of the pigeons which fortunately took the blow of the claw on its wing, a tremendous collision in mid-air; white pigeon feathers came floating down, like snow in May.

Starlit spring night. The dim light from a reading lamp, a comfortable armchair. What's good about living alone? No sounds of children shouting, or a mother crying. No dresses in the wardrobe. No bickering about the time and trivialities. No half-naked body on the left side of the bed. There's nothing good about living alone, apart from solitude on a quiet spring evening.

For various reasons he can't get to sleep in his own bed. Night after night he lies awake thinking the same thoughts over and over again. He tries to sleep on the sofa in the living room, but this migration from one room to another makes no difference, the thoughts that troubled him in the bedroom, trouble him in the living room too. Lack of sleep makes it impossible to concentrate, he can't face reading books, or newspapers. He can't hold proper conversations, he's testy and irritable, doesn't want to see his friends. He keeps himself to himself. His thoughts turn steadily blacker, for the first time he contemplates ending it all. He'll swallow a handful of sleeping pills, swallow them with water. But he wants to make one last journey, he's never been to Berlin. He's always had a hankering to see Berlin, and now he makes up his mind to go. He books a room in a hotel that's been recommended in a magazine: Askanischer Hof, in Kurfürstendamm.

To his great satisfaction the hotel is old-fashioned and threadbare, as if it belongs to a different age, as if now he's entered an era that predates his own. The hotel isn't devoid of a certain elegance; his room has large windows hung with thick, deep-red curtains. A lamp with a green shade provides a gentle, numbing light in the room. There's a writing table in front of the window which looks out over a quiet back garden. In the garden there's a beech tree. The bed is narrow with a frame of shiny metal, he's cocooned and safe in the bed. On the first evening, he falls asleep almost as soon as his head touches the pillow. He sleeps long and deeply. He sleeps almost continuously for eleven hours, until he's woken by the chambermaid who wants to clean and tidy his room. She knocks discreetly. He opens the door a fraction, asks her politely not to service the room for the next few days. I'm here to sleep, he says.